MW01278250

The Soldier, the Avatar, and the Holocaust:

WWII Germany, Jan.-May, 1945

RONNI SANLO

The characters and persons portrayed in this book are fictitious with the exception of some of my family members. Any similarity to a real person, living or dead, is coincidental and not intended by the author. Many of the events are also fictitious though most are based on actual events via researched materials.

ISBN:
ISBN-13: 978-0692757154
ISBN-10: 0692757155

Front cover and internal graphics:
Beth Muncy

Full cover design:
Barb Gottlieb
Gottgraphix.com

Rainbow Division and military photos courtesy of:
Suellen R. McDaniel, Editor
42nd Rainbow Division's *Rainbow Trail* and *Reveille*
and the
Lebman Family

Printed in the United States

Reviews

Up to 85 million dead. Six million Jews murdered. But why? What drove the atrocities of WWII? Beth, a teenage cosplay avatar meets up with her great-grandfather, then a 20-year old solider, to learn how he, the other soldiers, and the everyday people of European towns and villages in 1945 struggled to survive, connect, and find fragments of hope during a time of unimaginable suffering. Prejudice thrives in the fertile soil of rigid ideology. Sanlo, a gifted historian and storyteller, inspires readers of all ages to follow the pathway of humanity, respect, and dignity.

Judy Chiasson, PhD
Human Relations, Diversity & Equity
Los Angeles Unified School District

The Soldier, the Avatar, and the Holocaust brought me to tears. As a U.S. Army veteran, I was completely pulled into the story, and felt such compassion for Sandy. The book is extremely well written. Descriptions are excellent, and the rhythm of the writing is consistent throughout. And I learned so much!

Helen Ruth Schwartz
Author
US Army Veteran

Ronni Sanlo has written an extraordinary book! She has captured the realities of World War II simultaneously from the eyes of a young Jewish soldier who was actually there, and a modern day teen's perspectives! She obviously researched many facts about the progression of the war, especially of the 42nd Rainbow Division, as well as from the tender letters written by this young soldier to his new bride. This book should be recommended reading for all high school students to have a better understanding of what really happened in the holocaust, and to honor the words of "Never Again!

Barbra Miner
Psychologist/Retired

I hold a Ph.D. in US history and a master's degree in European history, both focusing on the social/cultural history of the 20th century I felt knowledgeable about how the average citizen responded to the vagaries and horrors of war, that is, until I read Ronni Sanlo's *The Soldier, The Avatar, and the Holocaust.* This book is an historical novel but she did not flinch on research. There are several explored themes including what happened to German children during war, the desire of the young Jewish soldier who is determined avenge the death of his extended family at the hands of the Nazis., and the need of the avatar to understand. This is an exciting book. Sanlo walks her readers through the war and through the eyes and ears of two young people from different centuries but of the same family. Where the 20th century soldier is accepting of the status quo in all things war, our 21st century time-traveller questions everything she sees, hears, and does. Imaginative, humorous, and compelling, this book will have a substantial impact on every person who reads it. A fascinating read indeed.

Dr. Regina Lark
History Professor
Pearce College, Los Angeles

This book transcends generations as the soldier/protagonist fights in the US Army during WWII while the student/Avatar fights her own personal war. From the perspective of this retired military person, Dr. Sanlo got the military piece right. It's an important read for people of all ages.

Jeri Neiberding
US Air Force/Ret

The Soldier, the Avatar, and the Holocaust:

WWII Germany, Jan.-May, 1945

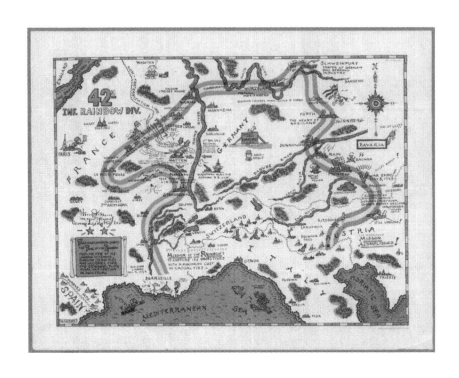

Route of the 42nd Rainbow Division

Europe, January–May, 1945

TO MY PARENTS

SANFORD (בשלום משכבך על נוח) AND
LOIS LEBMAN

AND

TO THE GENERATIONS OF THEIR
CHILDREN, GRANDCHILDREN, AND
GREAT-GRANDCHILDREN

Whoever survives a test, whatever it may be, must tell the story.

Elie Wiesel

Has the like of this happened in your days or in the days of your parents? Tell your children about it, and let your children tell theirs, and their children the next generation!

Joel 1:2-3
On the entrance wall of
Yad Vashem Holocaust Museum
Jerusalem

TABLE OF CONTENTS

THE RAINBOW FAREWELL

Dear Departed Rainbow Comrade:

It seems but a short time since you stood shoulder to shoulder with your buddies under that brilliant hued arc that stretched from New York to California, and the outskirts of Dachau to the city of Munich.

How well you remembered those days when so many of your comrades were called upon to make the supreme sacrifice. A friendship such as yours could only have been conceived in battle at a time when your lives depended so much upon one another.

It has been through the grace of God that you were given the privilege of continuing your comradeship these many years, and we are so proud of you. God gave you and your comrades a fellowship that has never been equaled, a fellowship of the Greatest Generation of Rainbow soldiers.

Your mission in following the Rainbow to its glorious end was not to find the proverbial pot of gold, but rather the noble purpose of bringing added glory to the Flag of our Country.

This you have done, and we salute you.

You have now answered the call of the Celestial Bugler. With silent marching feet you have enrolled in the Great Spirit Army of fellow Rainbowers. We pray that we, too, find the way some day, and assemble with you upon that Eternal Parade Ground, over the Rainbow.

Amen

Cpl. Sanford M. "Sandy" Lebman
42nd Rainbow Division, 222 Infantry
1st Platoon Cavalry, Reconnaissance
Serial Number 35236439
World War II
3/13/1925-1/31/2013

ACKNOWLEDGEMENTS

This has been a surprisingly accidental and deeply powerful work of love, created in teamwork with my family and supportive friends who were as excited as I about this project. I owe tremendous thanks beyond these mere words to:

My daughter, Berit Van Neste, for her research in family history and for asking the right questions at the right time. She provided nearly all of the early history of the immigration and documentation of her great-grand parents, Saul and Pauline Lebman;

My granddaughters, Beth and Callie Muncy, for teaching me about avatars and teenagers;

My son, Erik Sauls, for the many dinner discussions, readings, feedback, and loving support;

My sister, Barbra Miner and her husband Hal Miner who accompanied our parents to Dachau, Germany, for the 65th liberation memorial in 2010, and who shared their stories and photos with me.

My sister, Sherry Horwitz (בשלום משכבך על נוח) and her husband Barry Horwitz for their ongoing support for this project from the collation of the letters to conversations with me for clarity;

My brother, Len Lebman, and his wife Carole Rae Engstrom, for their enthusiastic support;

Suellen R. McDaniel, editor of the Rainbow Division's *Rainbow Trail* and *Reveille* newsletters, for sharing Rainbow history with me, and for being a tremendous resource during my initial research;

Rainbow Combat Photographer, Sgt. William R. "Hap" Hazard, whose photos appear in the *Rainbow Combat History of World War II*. Prior to his death, he gave permission for his photos to be used in any way that Suellen McDaniel saw fit. Suellen gave permission to me to use Sgt. Hazard's photos;

The authors of the *42nd Infantry "Rainbow" Division* (1946) memory book which provided initial information;

Kelsey Fuchs, Donor Services Coordinator, USO, for sharing dates and events with me about USO events in WWII Europe;

The people on the 42nd Rainbow Division Facebook page for their input, personal family stories, and the generous sharing of ideas - www.facebook.com/groups/42ndInfantryDivision;

Michele Patterson who shared her father Michael Patterson's letters with me. He proudly served in the 7th Army, 93rd Anti-Aircraft, T-5 Mechanic, and was at Dachau at the same time as my father;

My editors and critique partners Barbra Miner, Len Lebman, Erik Sauls, history professor Dr. Regina Lark, Jeri Nieberding (Air Force, Ret), and Dr. Kelly Watson.

My pal, Regina Lark, for her feedback and encouragement throughout this project and her tremendous support of every other cockamamie project I've initiated over the decades of our friendship;

My beloved partner, Kelly Watson, for her support of this ongoing project, for her feedback after reading, for the trip to Munich to see Dachau for myself, for understanding my need to write, and for her gracious heart and unending love;

Our four-pound Yorkie, Dooney Watson, who made sure I took breaks because he needed to be walked;

My mother, Lois Lebman, for lovingly (and surprisingly!) keeping all of Dad's WWII letters and artifacts intact. This is the first time she has shared her memories which are equally as important as Dad's. She has agreed to donate the letters and artifacts to the Jewish War Veterans History Museum in Washington D.C. where Dad's name already appears on their Wall of Honor, a gift to him from his children for his 75th birthday. With these artifacts intact, future researchers will read my father's story documented in his letters and perhaps understand some of the realities of the Holocaust; and finally to

My father, Sanford Lebman, who bravely did what he had to do in 1945 as a young soldier, living with the secrets his whole life, then suddenly sharing them every day (to anyone who would listen!) as an old man, and for allowing me to tell his story in my own way. He flew "over the Rainbow" on January 31, 2013 at the age of 87. He is dearly loved and deeply missed.

It took a village and a family to write this book… I am truly grateful beyond measure.

Ronni Sanlo

PREFACE

It was a typical balmy summer evening in Tampa, Florida, that June of 2009. My parents, Sanford and Lois Lebman, and I were visiting my daughter Beth, her husband Roy, and my teenage granddaughters Beth and Callie. Berit, the family historian, loved to hear her grandfather's stories of World War II and now she wanted her daughters to hear the stories as well. It took very little prompting to get my then-84 year old father to talk about his experiences as a soldier, though for over 60 years he never said a word, not once, about the war and his role in it. Ironically, though, my family attended the annual 42nd Rainbow Division reunion almost every year when my siblings and I were young, but somehow I never connected those reunions with my father actually *being* in the army nor taking part in the killing of others.

In the last few years of his life, though, Dad obsessed about his army years. He never missed a chance to talk about his role in the liberation of Dachau Concentration Camp or some of the more humorous military experiences of himself and his buddies, but he never spoke of killing people or of his buddies getting wounded or killed. Dad himself was wounded on three different occasions but spoke only about the wound he received at Camp Gruber, Oklahoma, while in basic training when someone accidentally pulled the pin on a live hand grenade. Dad covered the grenade with his helmet then fell on top of it, wounding himself but saving others from the errant grenade explosion.

As an old man, Dad wore his 42nd Rainbow Division cap with "WWII" on it everywhere—restaurants, airplanes, public places. It wasn't unusual for people to stop and thank him for his service. In fact, I saw it happen at a restaurant in Tampa that very morning in June, 2009. A young man in his twenties walked right up to Dad, shook his hand, thanked him for serving his country, and paid our check!

Back at the hotel, Berit began querying her grandfather. With Dad, all that was really needed was one well-placed question and he was off and running. Berit knew the right question.

"Pop, what was it like to liberate Dachau?"

Without hesitation he began to tell his story. Beth, then 14, and Callie, 11, listened intently as did Berit and Roy (Berit's husband is also an historian), along with Mom and myself. As Dad told the story—much of which I'd heard dozens of times over the last couple of years—he stumbled over some of the usual details. At 84, his memory was beginning to falter. Mom intervened.

"No, Sandy (Dad's nickname), that's not what happened. It was…" She'd remind him, he'd correct, then continue on, until the next stumble.

"Sandy, that's not right. It was…" He'd say something like, "Oh, yeah. Yeah. That's right." And continue.

After a few more stories and a couple more stumbles, Mom said, "Sandy, tell them about Frau Hauf."

I'd heard the Frau Hauf story many times, about how Dad was asleep in a bedroom in Frau Hauf's house in Germany and had almost shot her when she entered the room to bring more blankets. But this time he didn't remember the story. He didn't remember Frau Hauf. Mom's eyes moistened as she slowly shook her head and mouthed the words to me: *he doesn't remember.*

After one more tearful story prompt from Mom, I asked her, "Mom, how do you know all this stuff? You were back home in Ohio at the time."

"It's in the letters," she said matter-of-factly as she began shuffling a deck of Go Fish cards to play with Callie.

"Letters? What letters?" In my 62 years, I had never heard my mother mention letters. I had seen the 42nd Division photo book a few times over the years, but letters?

"The letters Dad sent to me when he was in Europe. He wrote almost every day."

"Mom," I could barely ask the question. "Do you still *have* the letters?"

"Sure!" she answered proudly. "I saved all of them! I have pictures and post cards and the *Hagaddah*, too!"

"*Hagaddah*?" I asked, wondering what on earth Dad was doing with the Passover prayer book in the midst of the war.

"Yes, for their Passover Seder in 1945, behind enemy lines. They had to write it themselves. I have it all."

The next month, July, I went to my parents' house in Ventura, California. Mom showed my sisters and me the letters and artifacts that she'd lovingly saved all these decades. My sisters—Sherry Horwitz and Barbra Miner—and I inserted all the letters into protective sleeves, collated them, and put them chronologically into four three-inch binders. It is primarily from those letters that this book is written, though certainly with a huge twist.

In the summer of 2011 my granddaughters Beth and Callie came to California for a couple of weeks to visit with the family and me. They're brilliant, passionate, interesting young women and we had terrific conversations, especially when we spent time with my son, Erik Sauls. Through those conversations it occurred to me that the story of WWII must be told in a way that young people like my granddaughters, as well as my generation of Baby Boomers, are equally able to find relevance and interest. It was with the input from my granddaughters that the story of the story was born.

This book is an historical novel. It's historical in that the information about the war in Europe, some of the people, and the liberation of Dachau are true based on my father's letters and the data I obtained from the National Military Archives in Baltimore, MD, as well as the Rainbow Division's newsletters and other academic sources. My father graciously allowed me to interview him many times. During what was to be one of our last sessions, I asked what the war was *really* like for him. For the first time, he said, "I tried to forget the bad parts and live life as best I could, but it always affected my family and me." He was diagnosed with post-traumatic stress disorder in 2008. He died in January, 2013.

This book is also a work of fiction because some of the stories about the soldiers and all of the stories about the avatar, of course, are entirely figments of that fertile field called my imagination. All names are fictitious except those of my father, my granddaughters, and my mother. All other names are based on the common names of the time and are not actual people. If someone appears familiar to a reader, it is entirely coincidental. The stories of the children who lived in the wartorn towns were created from the scant documentation of what life must have been like for them at that time. There is very little information about their experiences so I took what I could find and filled in the blanks which are likely not entirely accurate.

In 2013, Rhonda Fink-Whitman, director of *The Mandate Video* asked college students in Pennsylvania what they knew about the Holocaust. The sad, simple answer was *nothing*. They didn't know what it was, when it occurred, where it started, what country Hitler led, what concentration camps were, how many Jews were murdered, who else besides Jews were targeted, why the beaches of Normandy were stormed nor Normandy's location, what the tattoos on prisoners' arms were or what they meant, who Winston Churchill was, who the president of the United States during WWII was, who the Allies were, who Ann Frank was, nor what the yellow Star of David meant. They didn't know the definition of genocide even though it's happened in their lifetime.

In Rialto, CA, eighth-grade students were asked whether the Holocaust "was an actual event in history," or "merely a political scheme created to influence public emotion." After reviewing documents given to them by their teachers, many of the students argued against the validity of the Holocaust!

The fact that young people today don't know of the Holocaust is terrifying to me. This story must be told so that another Holocaust never happens again.

Prologue

On April 29, 1945, a 20-year old Jewish soldier in the 42nd Rainbow Division of the U.S. Army named Sanford "Sandy" Lebman ordered the driver of his M8 armored car to crash through the northwestern gate of Dachau Concentration Camp near Munich, Germany. Through letters, media research, and personal interviews, this is the mostly true story of a young soldier's experience during WWII.

This is also the story of a 17-year old time-traveling avatar named Beth, the soldier's great-granddaughter, who accompanies her great-grandfather through the last five months of WWII. That part, of course, is not true, *but could it have happened?*

1.

BETH: PROUD TO BE A NERD

Ms. Moore gave the weekend homework assignment to her senior history class. "Write a paper about the Holocaust. Make an argument as to whether the Holocaust was an actual historical event or a work of fiction created by Jews for political and monetary gain. I'm giving you some resources to consider." Ms. Moore handed out some papers.

"*Whaaaat?*" Beth was in shock as she spoke in a whispered tone to no one in particular. "Really??? We're supposed to decide if the Holocaust was real??? Moore's totally lost it this time!" Beth could barely breathe. Her anger was palpable.

"She calls these resources???!" Beth's exasperated whisper wasn't so quiet now. "Credible? One says Anne Frank faked her diary! Ms. Moore is the hoax, not the Holocaust. Next she's gonna ask us to debate whether 9/11 actually occurred!" Beth's voice became louder.

"Beth," said her girlfriend Nikki, "careful..."

Beth was fully agitated now. "The Holocaust *happened,* damn it!"

"Uh, *excuse* me, Beth. NOW what's your problem?" Ms. Moore was more irritated than usual with Beth who had an ongoing problem with staying tuned in to Ms. Moore's boring (and usually wrong) lectures.

Oh, hell, thought Beth. She loudly blurted, "This homework is just wrong! There's no academic value! It just legitimizes the hateful people who say the Holocaust didn't happen." Beth was furious, her head halfway hung on her chest but her words were well emphasized. Again with a raised voice, "If the Holocaust never happened, where the hell did six million Jews go???"

"That's *it*! *Out* of here, Beth. Take yourself and your, your whatever it is, your avatar thing and get OUT of my classroom!"

The bell rang as if to punctuate Ms. Moore's sentence. Beth and Nikki walked into the busy hallway.

"Beth, you've *got* to stop pissing her off. You're gonna fail. This is your friggin' senior year. Just do the work and keep quiet."

"I just can't help it, Nik. And *this* time friggin' Moore is way over the top! She tells us one thing, our great-grandfather tells us another. He was there, damn it! Who're you going to believe? Ms. Ignoramus is like a skinhead who thinks the Holocaust never really happened. But it did!"

Beth stopped walking, was thoughtful for a moment, then turned and looked directly into Nikki's eyes. She said in a near whisper, "Nikki, I gotta go. I need to see with my own eyes."

Nikki knew she couldn't stop her stubborn girlfriend. "Be careful, Beth. I'll cover for you."

"Thanks. My Pop is there. I'll be with him. I'll be okay. I owe you…"

My name is Elizabeth but I go by Beth. I'm 17 and a self-identified nerd, and proud of it! I go to public high school in St. Petersburg, Florida, that state where nearly every stupid thing in the news happens, so I prefer my computer world. The only class I liked in school this year was French, but my French teacher got fired half way through the year. I don't know why. It sucked.

My history class also sucks. *Seriously* sucks! So boring, and usually so wrong. The only way I made it through this far was to pretend my teacher was an idiot who was paid to teach us stuff backwards from the way they really happened. Sadly, though, that's exactly what she does. And then I usually get in trouble for trying to correct her. Aaaarrrggghhhhh! Why do I bother???

This is why I prefer my computer world. I can create my avatar and go wherever I want, anytime, in any century in the past. For you old folks, an avatar is a graphical computer repre-sentation of a character someone would like to be. (I warned you, I'm a nerd.) So my real teacher, the one I actually pay at-tention to, is Hidekazu Himaruya, the guy who created *Hetalia*. *Hetalia* is a satire where countries in World War II Europe are personified. *Hetalia* teaches that even though we're all different and come from different parts of the world, deep down we all have the same fears and desires for freedom. So countries are given personalities and names with specific clothing or cos-tumes. The interactions among the personified countries might be anything from romantic to make-believe which, really, I guess all of this is.

The best part, though, is the cosplay. I love cosplay! Co-splay is what happens when real people like my friends and I wear those personified-country costumes in our everyday life. So on any given day I could be dressed as the personification of Italy or Spain or Sweden or Germany, whatever I feel like. My favorite cosplay *Hetalia* character, though, is America, who is raised by the character England and later, of course, fights for independence. I told you...such a total nerd.

It's not a fad or anything new for me, my nerdiness. I've been like this for as long as I can remember. And if you think *I'm* weird, you should meet my family! *Damn!* My sister Callie, she's okay. She's kind of a nerd, too, so we have a lot in common and spend lots of time together. My parents are divorced. Big whoop. Like, whose parents *aren't* divorced? We live with our dad during the week and with our mom on weekends and most of the summer. My sister and I chose to live with dad because he's as big a nerd as we, maybe even bigger! Okay, he's, like, *huge!* Like on Halloween, well, *months* before Halloween, he begins construction of HellView, the best and scariest place in town! Right in our yard! Front and back! It's *waaay* cool! And he takes us and our nerdy friends to Comic-Con and Metro-Con and other awesome comic and gamer events.

My mom is a teacher. Fourth grade. In a Muslim school. She's scary smart and could probably be anything in the world, but she wanted to be a teacher. I'd hate to be in her class, though. I'm sure she's super strict. She's married to her second husband, who was her professor when she was in college. He's pretty smart, like she is, I'll give him that. But he's totally clueless about kids today. He thinks we should be perfect little children, exactly like he was back on the farm in Michigan about, oh, a thousand years ago. But he and mom take my sister and me to Disney World almost every weekend so I cut him some slack for that. So there's kind of a *small* cool factor with my mom and her husband because my sister and I *love* Disney World. I wear my cosplay clothes there and *always* see lots of people just like me. Disney World is *waaay* nerdier than people think!

My mom and her brother, my totally cool Uncle Erik who lives in Los Angeles, don't talk to my Grandfather Jake. There was some sort of huge family church thing about Uncle Erik being gay and mom being divorced. My grandfather's family is super right-wing religious. I heard that they left the Southern Baptist church a long time ago because it became too liberal. I don't get it. How can anyone be so stupid to just cut off family because of being gay or divorced? Hell, isn't *everybody* at least one of those????

Oh, it gets better. My grandparents divorced in 1979 when my grandma came out as a lesbian. She's absolutely the coolest grandma ever. She drives around in a purple golf cart, and she's a total warrior for social justice all over the country. And she thinks I'm the smartest, most terrific kid ever! Really! She tells me that all the time. Sometimes I even believe her. I just wish my teachers could see whatever it is my grandma sees in me. She wraps her arms around me and hugs me tight and makes me feel so safe. I may be getting older, I'm 17, but I always love that feeling.

When my grandparents divorced, my Grandfather Jake's family wouldn't let grandma see her own kids, my mom and Uncle Erik. Grandfather had custody because of my grandma being a lesbian. My mom lived with him, just like I live with my dad, but there aren't a lot of other similarities.... just enough to know that history repeats itself in some ways. I learned that through *Hetalia*. So Mom and Uncle Erik went for *years* without seeing their mother. Right! I mean, like, my coolest grandma! Crazy, huh? But they reunited with her when Mom and Uncle Erik were in their twenties, just a few months before I was born.

My grandma and her parents, my great-grandparents, live in California. My great-grandmother is 85. My great-grandfather—I call him Pop—is 86. They may be old but I actually remember my *great-great*-grandmother Mae who died just a few years ago at almost 103. We used to have big birthday parties for her every year. Her 100th birthday, I remember, was crazy fun! Lots of relatives from all over the country came to celebrate. That's when I realized that nerdiness is probably hereditary!

I love cosplay and *Hetalia*, like I told you. I live it every day, and I play at being different personified countries in Europe. My Pop, my great-grandfather, was actually in Europe during World War II. I was shocked when I learned that about him, and now I'm totally fascinated, especially after Ms. Moore's stupid assignment. I want to know more about what it was like for him and I want to know more about WWII. I didn't expect to be so involved in the actual Holocaust.

Last year I secretly started testing avatar development because I really wanted to travel back in time. I learned about DARPA, the Defense Advanced Research Projects Agency, which is the sort-of-secret research wing at the U.S. Department of Defense. They work on robots and avatars. See, an avatar partners with virtual reality to act as a person's surrogate in time-travel. That means my body stays here in a computerized bed, kind of like one of those tanning beds, which I actually use with my computer as my time machine, but my surrogate, my avatar, goes wherever I send it. That way, I'm not really in danger anywhere because I can wake myself up whenever I want. What's really cool is that right now DARPA has robots like Petman and AlphaDog to do the dirty work of war using visual sensors and vocal commands. But they're working on humans and telepresence which is another word for time-travel, and, really, they should hire me because, like, I can do that already. Really...

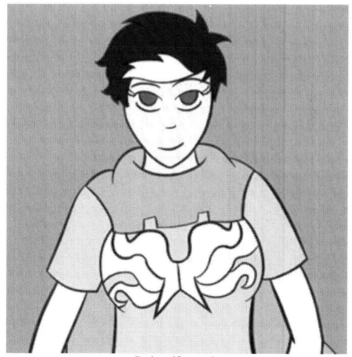

Beth, self-portrait

2.

YOU'RE IN THE ARMY NOW!

"Why are you crying, Dad?" asked 15 year old Sandy. His father was holding a letter in his trembling hand. Sandy had never seen his father cry before, no matter how frightful the situation. His father put the letter on the table for Sandy to read. It was from the CARE company that helps people in the United States send money to their relatives overseas. It was 1941 and Sandy's relatives lived in Poland. The letter read *Don't send any more money. There's no one left.*

"No one left, Dad? Where are they? Where'd they go?" asked Sandy, not understanding what the letter meant.

"Dead," said his father softly, his head hanging on his chest. "Killed... by... Nazis." His words, with his thick Polish accent, were quiet but like a soft growl through his clenched teeth. Sandy could hear the anger and the pain.

"Dead? No! Why, Dad?"

"Because we're Jews." Sandy's father walked away, into the privacy of the back room of the little grocery store the family owned, and sobbed.

Young Sandy could hear his father's immense sorrow. He vowed to avenge his family's deaths... just as soon as he was old enough to join the army.

———————

By April of 1940, Jews in Poland had been confined to ghettos as Germany was attempting to conquer all of Europe. United States General and Chief of Staff George C. Marshall initiated the expansion of the U.S. army which had fewer than 200,000 active duty soldiers. Germany had nearly three million.

By the spring of 1941, Hitler had ordered the extermination of all European Jews. The United States, maintaining an isolationist stance, did nothing until December 7, 1941, when Pearl Harbor in Hawaii was attacked by Japan. Germany sided with Japan and declared war on the United States which was then forced to act. By 1942, concentration camps—prisons for the purpose of killing Jews primarily but also homosexuals, physically challenged people, and many others—were in full operation throughout Germany and Poland. By the time Sandy turned 18 in 1943, old enough to join the army, over 56,000

Jews had already been killed in the Warsaw Ghetto in Poland alone, some of them Sandy's relatives.

Sandy was torn. He had just graduated from East Liverpool High School in Ohio. While he wanted to go into the army and do his duty to avenge his family against the murderous Nazis, he also wanted to go to Ohio State University where he had been accepted into the pharmacy program. The U.S. government, however, made the decision for him: Sandy was drafted in September of 1943.

Sandy told one of his friends, "My mother worries about everything. She's worried I'm gonna get killed. But I know what I need to do. Kill Nazis." Sandy had been a shy boy and was now a shy young man, overly concerned about his younger siblings, and worried about his own future. This bravado he exhibited was new, and it made him uncomfortable.

Sandy was sent to Camp Gruber in Oklahoma where he was inducted into the 42nd Rainbow Division, 222nd Infantry, G Company, 1st Platoon. He became a radioman with the Infantry's Reconnaissance unit, the Recons, and was assigned to an M8 armored car as a radio gunner. The Recons were the guys out in front of the other troops. They observed what was happening ahead of the front lines, decided what was needed, then radioed back to the command post—the CP. It was an extremely dangerous job.

Sandy was injured in a training pit at Camp Gruber when one of the guys accidentally pulled the pin on a live hand grenade then dropped it where the men were standing. Without thinking, Sandy threw his helmet down over the grenade then laid down on top of the helmet. When the grenade blew, Sandy was cut everywhere, with shrapnel deep in his upper torso. He was hospitalized for two weeks then sent home for a month-long convalescence furlough.

When he fully recovered and returned to duty, Sandy and his company prepared to go overseas. The train ride from Camp Gruber in Oklahoma to Camp Kilmer in New Jersey took three days. The train stopped in towns along the way where the soldiers had to get off the train, run a mile, do some exercises, then get back on the train. People came out to watch the soldiers and cheer them on. Everyone knew they were going to war.

Sandy's train arrived at Camp Kilmer in December 1944, where last minute details were completed: immunizations, the writing of Wills, connecting with the various religious personnel. Many of the guys, including Sandy and his three buddies Ken Ketchum, Dickie Wilson, and AJ Jackson, went into nearby New York City, the first time any of them had ever been there. Their last days in the States were filled with fun in the Big Apple. Fun to these young men meant drinking and carousing in the streets of New York City on New Years Eve, 1944.

Sandy was always focused on his family, but now he was a thousand miles from home with no family anywhere nearby. While he wasn't the kind of guy to just idly chat with strangers, he did develop a friendship with three other new draftees. Sandy knew no one when he arrived at Camp Gruber. He was processed and sent to his quarters. The tall skinny guy in the bunk above him jumped down.

"Hey. I'm Ketchum. Ken Ketchum, from Prineville, Oregon."

"I'm Sanford Lebman. From East Liverpool, Ohio. Nice to meet you, Ken. People call me Sandy."

"Sandy! Nice to meet you. Call me Ketch. That's what my friends call me. Guess we better get to be friends since we share this here bunk." Ketchum slapped the front post with his hat. "Where's East Liverpool, Ohio? I know where Ohio is but I never heard of East Liverpool."

"It's a small town on the banks of the Ohio River, across from Chester, West Virginia, just north of Wheeling."

The guy in the next bunk perked up. "Wheeling, West Virginia? Hey! I know where that is! I'm from Belmont, West Virginia, not too far away. Also a small town on the Ohio River. Population 899. I'm Richard Wilson. Dickie."

"899," chuckled Sandy. "East Liverpool has Belmont beat then. We've got about 2,200 people."

"So does Gainesville. Gainesville, Florida. That's where I'm from," said the guy from the bunk above Wilson in a deep southern drawl. "I'm Andrew Jackson, after the president, but call me AJ. Tell you guys the truth, I really don't want to be here."

"None of us do," said Ketch, "but we didn't have much choice, did we..."

"I want to be here," Sandy said, with no bravado in his voice, just determination. "I'm Jewish and some of my family was killed in Poland by the 'krauts. I'm gonna kill Nazis to get even."

Ketchum, Dickie and AJ looked at Sandy with shock.

"I never met a Jew, Sandy," said Ketch softly. "I hate that your family was killed. Just know I got your back, buddy."

"Yeah, Sandy, same here," said Dickie.

AJ, in his southern drawl, agreed. "Me, too, Sandy. We're gonna kill 'krauts with you, man. Damn..."

The men shook hands all the way around and began to get to know one another. They felt awkward at first, especially Sandy, but they bonded quickly and began their careers together as new soldiers in the 42nd Rainbow Division of the United States Army.

3.

THE RAINBOW

Rainbow Division insignia

The Rainbow Division was unique as it was made up of National Guard units from different states around the country. Its history began with the U.S. entry into World War I when individual states competed for the honor of sending their National Guard units to Europe. The government created a division composed of Guard units from twenty-six states and the District of Columbia. The unit was dubbed "Rainbow Division" during its organization at Camp Mills in New York, based on the observation by Chief of Staff of the Division, Colonel Douglas MacArthur. He said that the 42nd Division "stretched like a Rainbow from one end of America to the other." The adopted insignia resembled a red, gold, and blue rainbow.

The Rainbow Division was designed to quicken the deployment of United States troops to Europe in World War I because National Guard units could be activated and trained quicker than could units of new draftees. The pre-WWII regular army was small and, for the most part, unprepared for another war. Some National Guard units had had recent combat experience in the Mexican Border Operation of 1916-1917, but in reality, using the National Guard may have been partially politically inspired since it would likely evoke public support for the War.

When America entered the Second World War, the 42nd Division was re-activated as a full army division and not as the National Guard. The Division commander, Brigadier General Harry Collins, echoed MacArthur's sentiments on the 42nd Division's unique status when he said, "The Rainbow represents all the people of our country."

The three regiments of the 42nd Division and a detachment of the Division Headquarters arrived at Marseilles, France, on December 8, 1944, and became Task Force Linden. The Task Force entered combat in the vicinity of Strasbourg, France, on December 24, 1944. Defending a 31-mile sector along the Rhine River north and south of Strasbourg, the Task Force was fighting in the Battle of the Bulge. After finally beating back the German army, on January 24, 1945, Task Force Linden returned to the command post in Marseille and trained with the Division's replacement troops which had arrived the week before, on Jan. 16th. Sandy, Ketch, Dickie, and AJ were among those replacement troops.

On February 14, 1945, the Division entered combat, going on the offensive and creating and expanding bridgeheads across the Rhine River. Wertheim, Wurzburg, and Schweinfurt fell after hand-to-hand engagements, and soon Furth was taken as well. On April 29th, 1945, the 42nd Division liberated some 30,000 people from Dachau, the most notorious of the Nazi concentration camps. Passing through Munich on April 30th, the Division cut across the Austrian border north of Salzburg. WWII in Europe ended on May 8, 1945.

Sandy and the Rainbow Division experienced some of the fiercest battles of the entire war. Because of the tremendous loss of life among the soldiers, to boost morale, Major General Harry J. Collins, commander of the 42nd Rainbow Infantry Division, wrote to his men:

... From its inception, your Division has been extremely proud of its heritage and equally determined to add honor and glory to its already lustrous record. What you will do in combat is a foregone conclusion and presents no problem to me. Soldiers are imbedded in the spirit of the Rainbow, alert, proud, aggressive, disciplined and well trained with the chance to show their mettle. I have every faith and confidence in you. Soldiers of the Rainbow, carry on! The eyes of the world are upon you!

Harry J. Collins
Major General, US Army
Commander

By the end of the war, the 42nd Division had been the first to enter Germany, the first to break through the Siegfried line, and the first into Munich. Rainbow soldiers had seized over 6,000 square miles of Nazi-held territory and ended the war as occupation forces in Austria. The Division was deactivated in the spring of 1946. That's when Sandy and Ketch were allowed to return home. Richard "Dickie" Wilson and Andrew "AJ" Jackson didn't make it.

4.

December 1944

In 2009, Sandy's granddaughter, the family historian, asked, "Pop, did you know what was happening in Europe before you got there with your unit? Did you know what you were getting into?" Sandy was emphatic, even after 65 years. "Yes. We were losing soldiers there. I was a Recon and knew I would be out in front in an armored car. I liked that. I had the first shot at killing Nazis."

In reality, Sandy had no idea what he was getting into that December of 1944. The largest and bloodiest battle of WWII in Europe, the Battle of the Bulge, was under way, and the first wave of the 42nd Rainbow Division was getting clobbered. Nineteen thousand young men died. Another fifteen thousand were taken prisoner.

During the freezing morning of December 16, 1944, over 200,000 German troops and nearly 1,000 tanks launched Hitler's last big attack. The German army struck in the Belgium Ardennes Forest, a seventy-five-mile stretch of dense woods with few roads. Four inexperienced battle-worn American divisions, in desperate need of rest, were attacked. At the first assault, the Germans broke through the American front and surrounded most of the divisions, seizing vital crossroads and advancing toward the Meuse River, which created the bulge that gave the battle its name. The men of the Rainbow Division were sitting ducks.

Stories of the massacre spread. The British waited nervously to see how the Americans would react to this full-scale German offensive. Even American civilians who had thought that victory was finally near were startled by the Nazi onslaught.

Reinforcements were rushed in to stop the German penetration, and soon Gen. George Patton's Third Army was battling the German flank. Within days, the Third Army, trudging through deep snow and dense woods, attacked vigorously until the bulge was shrunk and the front restored. Hitler would never again launch an offensive on such a large scale. British Prime Minister Sir Winston Churchill stated, "This is undoubtedly the greatest American battle of the war and will, I believe, be regarded as an ever-famous American victory." Indeed, the

33

Battle of the Bulge has been called the greatest fight in American military history.

———————

The replacement troops of the Rainbow Division were about to be deployed overseas. Nineteen year-old Sandy and his young buddies were among those about to ship out. Sandy wrote to his 18 year-old bride, Lois, back in East Liverpool, who he hadn't seen in over a month. The letter was dated December 24, 1944, New York City:

My Darling Wife,

Well, here I am in the East. I can't tell you where so let's not get inquisitive. We left Oklahoma Wednesday and traveled for three days and three nights and now we're here. The trip wasn't so bad. We had Pullman cars and all modern conveniences. In fact, we were even served our meals in our seats. How do you like that for luxury?

You know, we were in Pittsburgh for six hours yesterday. Just imagine, so close to home yet so far away, but if we get a pass of any length of time, I'm going to try to come home. When I get your letters they certainly bring up my morale considerably.

What have you been doing lately, that is, in the line of recreation? I imagine there should be some ice skating and so forth, and I also hope that you're having a very pleasant holiday, Darling, considering everything, maybe next year we'll be able to celebrate together. We can hope, anyhow, can't we?

We start our processing today. It's supposed to take three days and after that I don't know what we do. I guess I'll just have to wait and see. That's one thing I don't like about the army. You never know what you'll do next or when you'll do it. I sure wish I had some idea.

Well, Darling, I guess I'd better close for now but I'll write again later. Give my love to everyone. So until later, Darling, I remain

   Your loving hubby,
   Sandy

Sandy and Lois had known one another since they were children. In 1934, when Lois' father was transferred to East Liverpool, Ohio, the first thing the family did after finding a place to live was to join the local synagogue. Lois was eight years old and Sandy was nine when they met in the synagogue's Sunday school program.

Sandy's parents, who fled from Poland to the United States in the early 1900s, owned a grocery store in the east end of town. Lois's parents, transplants from nearby Pittsburg, Pennsylvania, managed the S&S Shoe Store downtown. Both Sandy and Lois worked for their parents when they were each tall enough to reach the counters to help the customers. After graduating from high school in 1943, they each had intentions of going to college, but Lois had to put her college dreams on hold because her mother's failing health used up what little money was available to her. Since she had to stay home to care for her father and younger brother, she took a job at the East Liverpool First National Bank. Sandy was drafted into the U.S. Army.

They were married on April 16, 1944.

December 31, 1944
My Dearest Darling Wife:

Well, Happy New Year, Darling, since this is New Year's Eve. I guess that's just about the appropriate thing to start a letter off with. Don't you? You don't know how close you came to spending New Year's eve with me, darling, if only I could have gotten a phone call through we would have been together. But because of circumstances beyond my control I was unable to contact you. I guess I'll be in Times Square when the bell starts ringing tonight and I sure wish you would be with me. Maybe next year we'll have more luck and we may be able to get together.

We just got paid, Darling, and just guess how much I draw. All the way to $6.10. Just imagine. I think I'll go to town and really get stewed. In New York, that'll buy at least one drink. The other night when we were there we ordered five beers. There were five of us and they cost us $2.50. I made sure that it took only one beer to make me drunk. This month you get $80. It'll be in two separate checks or maybe you'll only get $50 and next month get a check for $50 and one for $60. At any rate, you'll get $80 a month from now on.

Don't forget to let me know where you spent New Year's Eve and all of that. I'll also let you know how things go at Times Square.

For a change today they let us sleep in, that is until 10:00 when we got paid. It really felt good, too, but no matter how long they let you sleep, you still hate to get up when they want you to.

I guess I'd better close for now, so until later, I remain,

Your loving hubby,

Sandy

Sandy and the Rainbow Division replacement troops shipped out for Europe the next day, January 1, 1945.

5.

THE MEETING ON THE SHIP

On January 1, 1945, Liberty ships sailed out of New York Harbor past the Statue of Liberty, carrying the 42nd Rainbow Division replacement troops to Europe.

Liberty ship, WWII

From Camp Gruber, the soldiers were sent to Camp Kilmer, New Jersey, 32 miles from New York City, which was the largest military staging area in the United States. The soldiers were warehoused there until they embarked on the ships that would carry them across the ocean.

The gigantic Liberty ship USS William Rogers departed from the North River Buck Terminal in New York on January 1, 1945. Liberty ships were cargo ships that had been quickly built, in about 24 days each, for the purpose of taking troops to Europe or Japan during WWII. Five thousand soldiers were herded like cattle through the large square door in the side of the ship. Each man carried a 100-pound duffel bag, a bedroll pack, a rifle and a steel helmet. The troops, mostly young draftees, found themselves below decks in rooms with 200 other men, with narrow individual bunks and thin mattresses, scratchy sheets and hard pillows. Daily training of physical exercise and three hours of lecture instruction were supposed to take place, but the seas became rough very quickly. Seasickness overcame nearly all of the men soon after they left New York. There were some days when it was all the soldiers could do to stand upright and walk, but the waves of nausea stopped them from doing much more than breathe. The ocean crossing took longer than expected to avoid areas that might have enemy attack-ships, and the seasickness lasted for much of the voyage.

Between the nausea and the stench from it, eating, training and recreation were not high on anyone's list of things to do. The seasickness made them miss home, and morale immediately hit bottom only days out to sea. The popular songs of the day, like *I'll Be Seeing You, Dearly Beloved,* and *Sentimental Journey,* were played repeatedly. The lonely, frightened cries of the young men could barely be heard above the constant hum of the ship.

Once on board, Sandy followed the men in front of him single file through a maze of hatches and companionways until he reached his assigned bunkroom. The area looked like a forest of steel pipes which supported canvas-strip bunks. Each bed, or more accurately hammock, was two feet wide by six feet long. Only two feet separated the hammocks above and below, tiered four high. The man in the uppermost hammock stared directly into rows of pipes immediately above his face. The men in the first, second, and third tier bunks had to try to avoid the indentation made by the body of the man above them, adjusting positions for adequate clearance. The aisles between the hammocks were narrow and crowded with packs and gear. The men were always climbing over something.

Sandy's bottom bunk was in a room on the deck just below the waterline. Each bunk had sheets, towels, a blanket, and a bucket. Sandy wondered what the bucket was for when he saw the accommodations but quickly forgot about it when he went back up to the ship's deck.

The USS William Rogers weighed anchor and set sail for a location unknown to the soldiers. The men didn't know where they were being sent, and many would never return. The ship joined a convoy of ten other similar ships carrying more replacement troops. The convoy was on its way to Marseilles, France, escorted by five combat vessels.

The waters were calm when the ship left New York. Sandy, who had never seen the ocean, watched the waves gently roll towards the ship as they passed the Statue of Liberty then on to the open ocean.

Sandy was amused by the flying fish that traveled alongside the ship. They lifted out of the water and sailed along for several yards before diving back down into the waves. Sandy was mesmerized by how the ocean changed color as the ship moved along, how the white caps of the waves splashed against the sides of the ship, and how the cold winter wind and the bright sunshine collided on his body. Sandy was fascinated with how the waves grew until a giant wave broke over the bow of the ship. The waves were quickly gaining in size and strength as the blue sky turned to an angry gray. The powerful waves began to push one side of the ship and then the other, causing the ship to roll hard each way. It was only the second day out at sea and Sandy became horribly seasick, as did nearly every other person on the Rogers.

Jan. 11, 1945
My Darling Wife:

I guess this is the eleventh. I wouldn't swear to it though because I've been so sick and dizzy ever since I got on this boat that it isn't even funny. Have you ever heard of seasickness, Darling? Well, I hope you never get as sick as I was. I'm feeling a bit better now though. I'm getting used to it. We're still out at sea. I don't know when you'll get this letter. We can't mail letters until we get to our destination wherever that is and I hope you haven't worried too much about not hearing from me because it wasn't my fault. If there was any way possible I could have communicated with you, believe me I would have done it.

They have made this trip as comfortable as possible under the crowded conditions and such. When we got on the boat the Red Cross was there with donuts and coffee and candy for all of us, and while we're out at sea they have made it possible for us to get books and magazines to read. They gave us little bags with shaving equipment, cigarettes, and candy and other things, and today we each got two packages of Raleigh's with the compliments of General Motors, so you see, Darling, there are some people that do share in trying to make us comfortable and happy.

I'll write to you again tomorrow, Darling. That'll give me something to do and it will also at the same time let you know that I am thinking about you continuously night and day, Darling.
Your loving hubby,
Sandy

Sandy climbed into his netted bunk, knowing he was going to be terribly ill and grateful that he was on the bottom of the column of four bunks. He quickly became so sick that he could barely remember where he was or how he got there. He now understood the reason for the bucket. *Vomit.* "Sick... as... a... damned... dog.... " Sandy said aloud to himself. "Why... am... I... here?... To... kill..." *Vomit.* "Nazis."

"Yuuucckkkk!!!!"

"Huh??" Sandy thought he heard a small voice that sounded like it belonged to a...a...girl? "Who said that? Someone there? God, I'm so sick, I'm hearing things."

"I said, yuuuucckkk!! You barfed...everywhere. It stinks!" said the voice.

"Can't help it. So damned seasick..... Wait!" Sandy attempted to look up from his bucket. "Who's there?" He tried to look around but his energy was sapped. It was all he could do to take off his smelly shirt. He lay there in his white t-shirt and olive uniform pants which he simply could not remove. His shoes were somewhere nearby, he hoped.

"Me. *I'm* here," a girl's voice said with announcement.

Great, thought Sandy. *Now I'm hallucinating besides being sick.* "Who *are* you? And *where* are you?" Sandy asked, his voice and movements weakened from the nausea.

"I'm Beth. Beth America. Over here. On your left shoulder."

Sandy turned his head, slowly. The voice belonged to a teensy tiny teenaged girl dressed in some kind of military garb: a dark brown leather bomber-type jacket and light brown military style slacks. Sandy was both surprised and curious, knowing he was in the midst of a giant sea-sick-induced fantasy. He studied her as best he could under the circumstances of the pounding sea and his gurgling stomach. He noticed that a "50" on a round white background was affixed to the upper left jacket pocket. A white skinny airplane was on her left upper sleeve.

A white shirt and brown gloves completed the military-style outfit. The tiny girl, though obviously nearly an adult, jumped down and sat on the edge of Sandy's pillow. Sandy was pretty clear now that he had fully lost it.

"Okay, I *know* I'm sick 'cause now I'm hearing *and* seeing things. And this boat is still rocking...Ohhhhh......."

Beth, self-portrait

The waves were slopping over the sides of the USS William Rogers, and the other 5000 soldiers were no better off than Sandy. He gathered his wits enough to see the four-inch tall uniformed girl now on his pillow, convinced that he was so sick that anything was possible.

"Who are you again?" Sandy asked, unsure of his sanity.

"Beth America."

"What's a Beth America?"

"Not *what*, Pop...*who*." She was getting a bit exasperated.

"Pop? What's a Pop?"

"*You* are. You're my great-grandfather. We call you Pop."

"Your, uh, *great*-grandfather? But I'm only 19! And I don't have kids! Heck, *I'm* just a kid! This is getting bad..." Sandy trailed off, now worried about his mental condition. His physical condition was already shot to hell.

"No, not so bad really. It just means you don't die here. You don't die fighting. The good news, Dude, is that you get to be really old." Beth laughed.

"Okay. I like that," said a weak Sandy. "Who are you again? And where'd you come from?"

"I'm Beth America. It's my cosplay name. I come from the year 2017."

Sandy looked baffled. "Cosplay?" He missed the 2017 part.

"Yeah. It means costume play. That's why I'm dressed this way. I'm dressed as the personification of the United States of America, so I'm Beth America. Get it?"

Sandy was completely lost. "No."

Beth continued. "My name is Beth. Right now, I'm 17 and it's 2017 in my world. I'm here because I can time-travel. I needed to come here, to go through Europe with you during the war."

Sandy was certain about his hallucinations now but decided to play along. "So how do you do the time travel thing? I don't think that's possible, just movie fantasy stuff."

"That's true in your real time of 1945, but not in mine...well, for some people. I'm actually an avatar, a digital persona that I can create and manifest so I can travel back in time without putting my real 2017 body in too much danger."

"Yeah, well, in my world it's 1945 and I'm sicker than I've ever been... but it's good to know I make it through the war. Right now I'd just be happy making it through this voyage." *Vomit!*

Beth jumped out of the way.

Sandy leaned on his elbow, looked at Beth, and thought more about what he'd just heard. "Wait!!" *Oh sweet disbelief!* "Great-granddaughter? Really? I don't believe a word you're saying, of course, or even understand any of it, but I'm sick enough to play along. And what's a dude? And..." Dry heaves. "What's your name again?"

Beth laughed. "You'll ask your family that often in about 65 years! Memory issues. My name is Beth. A dude is just a guy. Just a generic nickname, kinda like buddy. And right now I'm not really me, as I told you. I'm my avatar. I came back to the past to try to find out about the Holocaust and why people go to war. Why do people go to war, Pop? What are you doing here?"

He knew he was sick and hallucinating, but she was cute, and he was kind of a flirt in a shy sort of way. And he was feeling very alone and scared. He was glad for the company even if she wasn't real.

"I dunno. I guess most of us are here because we got drafted and now it's our job to protect our country?" It was more of a question than an answer. He missed the part about the Holocaust, a word that hadn't been used yet in Sandy's day.

"Is that really why you're here, Pop?"

"Pop. I like that. No... well, yeah, I guess. I got drafted. But I think I'm here because many of my...uh, *our*... family members from Poland were killed by the Nazis. I plan to avenge their deaths. Hitler is killing Jews. We're Jewish." Sandy dry-heaved again. "Ooooooo....... I feel so woozy.... I can't believe I'm talking to a minia-ture...something. A cute girl but you sure are little. Who are you again? And how did I end up with a-a great-granddaughter?" He chuckled as he coughed. At least the vomiting seemed to have ceased.

"I'm Beth, the granddaughter of your oldest daughter. We have kind of a big family."

"Oh, God... Okay, let's say you are who you say you are. Is my daughter as little as you?" Sandy, who never thought about having children, now seemed to be concerned about genetics.

"No, and I'm not little, either, in real life. I'm here as my avatar, my not-real person, so I can be any size I want. My plan is to stay small and be attached to you here on your left shoulder and in your left jacket pocket while you're in the war." Beth paused to think for a mo-ment then breathed a heavy sigh. "I just don't get why people hate each other, Pop. I understand your anger and desire to avenge the deaths of your, our, family. It's the whole war thing. I want to learn firsthand if I can, and I want to be connected to you here."

"Do you know anything about what's going to happen?" Sandy was beginning to take Beth seriously, thinking maybe she had more powers and knew more than she let on.

"I can't predict anything specific. I really only know what I learned in my history class, which I suspect was totally wrong. And I know we win the war but not until after thousands of American soldiers and lots of other people are killed. You don't die, of course, but it's gonna be hell. Trust me on that one!"

Somehow, he did.

Feeling exhausted from all the vomiting, Sandy said, "I gotta sleep. Oh-oh... I think I'm gonna throw up again. Ohhhhh..." Beth hung on to Sandy's shoulder while he heaved again but no vomit. *There must be nothing left in him*, she thought to herself, grossed out by all the vomit in the bucket. *If I can't deal with this, I'm sure not gonna be able to deal with the actual war.* She hung on to Sandy's shoulder while his body writhed from the nausea.

"Cigarette. I need a cigarette." Sandy took out a Camel and offered one to Beth. Beth thought he'd fallen asleep.

"You seriously smoke those things?" she asked. "They'll kill you!"

"Hell, I'm about to go fight a war in a place that I know absolutely nothing about. I could die there, regardless of what you say. I'm not worried about a cigarette killing me. Anyway, the ads on the radio say that nine out of ten doctors smoke Camels. Can't be all bad." Sandy chuckled. He saw that Beth and the cigarette were about the same size.

Exasperated, Beth said, "Dude, cigarettes are killers. Really. And didn't you hear me? I'm your *great-granddaughter*, which means you don't die because you have to go back home to...uh....where are you from anyway?

"East Liverpool, in Ohio."

"Yeah, East Liverpool, Ohio, to make babies with Gran-Gran."

"Who?"

"Gran-Gran. Your wife. Lois. My great-grandmother."

"Right," Sandy said as he fell asleep.

Beth wondered: *How can you hate someone so much that you want them dead? How can you hate so deeply just because of who someone is? Why do some people hate Jews? Because we're different? Are we so powerful as a people that they're frightened of us? What is so different?"*

She didn't understand....yet.

———————————

When Beth transformed into the avatar and headed for Europe, she knew she'd land on her great-grandfather's ship. The fact that she actually landed on his shoulder in his bunk was perfect! Realizing her small size, she decided that the best place to stay during her, uh, visit, would be in the upper left pocket on Sandy's jacket. It was warm in there, and she could hear and see whatever she wanted. And she some-how felt safe in there, next to her Pop's beating heart. She made herself at home.

Sandy, of course, thought Beth was an hallucination so he kept her presence to himself, not sharing with his buddies that he had a companion riding in his pocket. *Of course*, he thought, *if they think I'm mentally unstable, maybe they'll send me home. But then I couldn't kill Nazis.*

6.

JANUARY 1945:

WELCOME TO THE WAR

Once the Atlantic was crossed, the USS William Rogers sailed through the Strait of Gibraltar and into the calm waters of the Mediterranean Sea. Motion sickness subsided, and the men cleaned their disgusting bunk areas. On the main deck they were greeted with the crisp cold air of winter, the sky a bright blue and not a cloud in sight. The sun shone brightly on The Rock. It was impossible to fathom that only a few hundred miles to the north, soldiers like themselves were engaged in the deadly Battle of the Bulge.

Jan. 16, 1945
My Dearest Darling Wife:
Have you noticed the date on this letter, Darling? So you see, I still remember. I'll never forget. Nine months ago today. My, that was a beautiful day, wasn't it? Everything seemed to fit in perfect.

Beth interrupted Sandy's writing. "What happened nine months ago, Pop?"

"Lois and I got married," he replied, only mildly annoyed at the interruption. He continued to write.

Last night I saw Tale of Two Cities. *It was really a good show. I had seen it once before and I read the book, but I saw it again anyhow. Have you read the book, Darling? It's about the French Revolution.*

This morning, the way the fellows were jumping out of their sacks and getting dressed so early you'd think we had just arrived back in America, but it was because the ship was passing some land. I'm not allowed to tell you where we are but it was worth seeing. I'll try to tell you more about it in the future. Until later, Darling, I'll close with
Your loving hubby,

46

"What IS that?!" Beth had seen the Rock of Gibraltar only once, a photo in a geography book. The concept of its reality and location never occurred to her.

"That's the Rock of Gibraltar," whispered Sandy, feeling the awe of his surroundings. "I read about it in school and always wanted to see if it looked as good in person as it does in the books. It's even better…"

"I've seen some great places in the U.S. but this is totally cool," responded Beth.

"So you've traveled around the U.S.?" asked Sandy. Then he corrected, "Well, I guess you can since you made it over here in some magical way. I still think I'm dreaming you up. I have a feeling that's what happens when someone is homesick bad. He creates imaginary friends."

"No…I'm real. Just different. And yes, I've traveled a lot because I live in Florida, you and Gran-Gran and my grandma and my Uncle Erik live in California, and I have cousins in Washington D.C."

"No. I live in East Liverpool, Ohio," countered Sandy.

"Well, you do right now…" responded Beth. She didn't want to give him too much information about the future. Beth stopped, thought for a moment, then asked, "Uh, Pop? How are you feeling now that we're getting closer to landing?"

"I'm not looking forward to what lies ahead here except to kill the Nazis who killed my family. It's that simple. That's why I'm here. I told you that." Sandy was determined.

"I don't know, Pop. It seems like there should be more to it than that. I mean, like, that's important and all, though I'm still not sure about the revenge factor, but there's just got to be more. Look at these guys here with you. They're not Jewish. Hell, they don't even know any Jews but you! But here they are. Like, why would people fight and die for something they know nothing about?"

"How about for a person's country, for freedom, for liberty? I don't know. But not for me. My family was killed. I can't stand by and let it go. I have to do something. That's what makes this okay for me. That's it." Sandy was unwavering. It almost seemed to Beth that Sandy just didn't really want to know more. He had a job to do, a personal mission, and he was going to do it. Citizen soldier.

"Wow!" She whispered to no one in particular.

The USS William Rogers entered the harbor at Marseille, France. The men remained on board the ship overnight as they prepared to disembark. The weather had changed by the time they got to Marseille, and the blue skies of Gibraltar morphed into the fury of winter. The next day they left the ship on foot and by motorcade to their temporary station at Command Post 2—called CP2—a staging area two miles northwest of Calais, France.

After unloading baggage and equipment in the rain and cold and mud, the fatigued troops pitched their two-man tents on a treeless, wind-swept plateau. The weather made it tough to prepare vehicles or any of the equipment. There were no hot meals for the first two days until the kitchen equipment was unloaded and put into operation. Their food was K-rations, those color-coded bland card-stock packaged meals: Brown for breakfast, green for lunch, blue for dinner. Inside each box was a plain tan box, coated in wax to keep the contents waterproof. The breakfast box contained a small can of eggs and bacon chips, a pack of crackers, a small pack of instant coffee, a small pack of lemonade, some matches, and a pack of four cigarettes. The lunch and dinner packages were similar except they had cans of meat and cheese with bacon bits.

Yummy, thought Beth facetiously. Sandy ate everything without complaint. After trying to keep down meals on the high sea, Sandy thought it would almost be a new experience to eat without losing it.

CP2 was a rude introduction to Europe and a foreboding of the bone-chilling cold and wet days and nights to come. Red Cross tents were set up where soldiers could get coffee or cocoa and have a warm place to write letters. This was different from the world the soldiers left only two weeks before. The war was real. German planes sometimes flew in their direction at night, so there were blackouts and ear-splitting anti-aircraft gun noise. Each time planes drew near, the troops spread out, dug foxholes, and took defensive measures. There now seemed to be some purpose in the required training they were experiencing.

Command Post 2

A bitter wind was blowing. The temperature was near freezing. Sandy blew into his hands to try to fight off the cold as he and Ketch set up their small tent and situated their belongings. By the time darkness fell Sandy and all the other newly arrived troops realized how exhausted they were. There was a blackout in the camp at night so they wouldn't become targets for German planes, which petrified the new arrivals. Sandy crawled into his pup tent, not missing the rolling motion of the ship, and quickly fell asleep. The next morning came early and fast, and now the war was a reality. There was an intense training program for the newly arrived troops, and they were reminded that their letters home would be censored. The army didn't want them to send information that would inadvertently jeopardize their positions.

The men were issued ammunition for their M-1 rifles, a full field pack, two extra blankets, and a mattress cover.

"What on earth is that for?" asked Beth, wondering about the mattress cover.

"Damned if I know," replied Sandy. "They never mentioned it in training."

Sandy tented with his pal, Ketchum. He didn't tell Ketch about Beth. He just let him think he talked to himself...a lot.

"Hey, Ketch, what's this for?" Sandy held up the mattress cover.

"Damned if I know, Sandy, but I have a feeling we're gonna find out."

Sandy had guard duty the second night ashore. He bundled up in his wool uniform and thick jacket that had been issued earlier in the day. The cold bit through the fabric. As he shivered, he suspected there would be many more cold nights ahead. At least there was plenty of time to think when the camp was quiet in the blackness of night. When guard duty was over, Sandy quickly made his way back to his tent and fell into his bedroll for some sleep. After a schedule of being on and off guard duty for a couple of days, Sandy finally had time to sit down and get another letter written.

Sandy wrote a few letters home to Lois. Beth sat on his shoulder and watched him write. His writing was rather elegant, she noticed, especially for a man. He spelled out everything: *twenty* for *20* or *ten o'clock* instead of *10:00*. For Beth, the concept—and the time it took—to write letters was foreign. In 2017 it was enough to text and receive immediate response, the whole process of which took maybe 60 seconds. Anything more than that was too slow for her. It took a long time to write a letter, especially with those awful little pencils! The thought of it just made Beth's hand hurt! And then to have to wait—what? weeks over here?—for a response! No way could Beth understand communications without computers. She was observing it but she didn't get it, and she sure didn't like it.

"You keep writing these letters, Pop, but you haven't received any back yet. Isn't that, like, frustrating? And how does Gran-Gran know where to send the letters so they get to you?" Beth was concerned and confused.

"Well.... how else would you suggest I send my thoughts to her?" Sandy was perturbed. It was tough enough to get his thoughts on paper. He never needed to do that before. And now this little whatever-she-is is annoying him about it.

"Yeah, okay. Sorry. I'm used to doing things much, much quicker, on computers and iPads and iPhones."

"Huh...???"

"Never mind. You'll never get it. Lois will, but you won't."

Sandy still thought Beth was a figment of his imagination and just something he conjured up to help with the homesickness. But he knew if he were conjuring up a woman, it sure wouldn't have been his great-granddaughter! Betty Davis maybe, Carole Lombard for sure, Jane Russell absolutely, but a great-granddaughter??? Then he chuckled to himself because he realized that he hadn't conjured up his new wife just now. *Nah*, he justified to himself, *I wouldn't bring her to this miserable place.* So he accepted the fact that this vision of Beth America, whatever she was, was simply company. No questions asked.

Jan. 23, 1945
My dearest darling wife;

I'll try to write to you again tonight from my tent but it's so cold to write without gloves on that it isn't even funny. But I'll put up with it just so I can write to you. Today I sent you a cable. You'll probably get it in about six days after I send it but it's the fastest possible way that I could get any word to you so I sent it. I haven't gotten any mail yet but I sort of expect some tomorrow because the mail started to come through today. I hope that you've been receiving my mail regularly.

All day today we didn't do much more than just clean our guns. I guess it's true when those fellows told me that you have it easier overseas than you do in the states. One reason for that is that it's been too cold to do anything here.

You know, darling, it doesn't seem as though I am out of the USA except that I can't call you or have you come to see me and a few other things like that. But whenever you start thinking about home and how far away we are it really hurts. Every night I lay there in my tent. I can just lay there and I can see you, believe it or not, and I even talk to you, although you can't hear me. You answer me back because I can hear your voice so distinctly. Strange isn't it darling? I can't wait until I get home and hold you in my arms again, darling. It seems as though it has been years and in reality it's only been six weeks. That is even a long time. I guess I have to close for now darling but I'll write again tomorrow, and don't forget to think about me occasionally and remember I love you very dearly.

> *Your Loving Hubby,*
> *Sandy*

"Pop, when you write your letters, why don't you write about what's really going on here? The weather sucks, the food's awful, the guys are already a hot mess. Everyone's scared and homesick, and the fighting hasn't even started for you yet. Your letters are way too Mr. Nice Dude."

"Didn't you hear them the other day when we arrived? We're not allowed to write about where we are or what we're doing. The censors would just cut that stuff out of the letters before they get sent, and..."

"Wait! Whoa!" interrupted Beth indignantly. "The censors? Your letters are censored? Like, someone *reads* every letter before it gets mailed? Damn!!!"

"Damn? Beth! I never heard a woman say *damn* before!"

"Well, then, damn again! Censors? That's a huge violation of your privacy!" Beth was truly shocked that letters were censored by the military, and Sandy was still in shock from hearing a female curse.

"Okay, it's like this, see...if we say where we are and what we're doing, the enemy could get the letters and counterattack or whatever. So we have to be careful until after the fact. Understand? It's a safety thing for us. And anyway, I don't want Lois to worry about anything. I worry enough for both of us."

"What do you worry about, Pop? I already told you that you survive."

"I guess, but I still wonder what's going to happen. We've never been under fire. We were told it would be easy, that we just go in and shoot Germans and move on. But somehow I don't think so..."

Each day during the ensuing weeks the troops trained in the hills of CP2 near Calais, applying and reviewing the principles of combat tactics. They stood inspection of weapons and equipment and were given clothing and supplies. The weather made life miserable. It was too cold to snow, the nights going way below zero and the days weren't much better. The cold permeated everything including their morale.

After two weeks at CP2, they received orders to move. They loaded equipment onto old train boxcars which had been used in WWI, called "40 and 8." They could hold 40 men and eight horses. The weather had warmed a little, to the upper 30s, but then the rain began.

"It's bad enough eating in the rain, " Sandy complained, "but wet powdered eggs is just awful!"

"Iccckkkk...," was all Beth could say.

Boots got wet and muddy during the day and cold and stiff at night while the men slept. They had to dig trenches around their tents to keep the rainwater from running in. Those mattress covers, they discovered, were used to keep their blankets dry. Sandy folded his blankets, put them into the mattress cover, then crawled inside to sleep. Luckily, Beth was always toasty at night, wrapped up in Sandy's left pocket.

Beth, usually too nerdy to be a fashionista, noted what the soldiers were wearing, mainly so she could be better with cosplay when she went back home to 2017. While nothing was stylish, neither was Beth, so she felt at home in the company of these olive-drabbed men. The uniform that Sandy's unit was given was made of basic wool, a field jacket with a wool overcoat, and a helmet with web gear. The helmet weighed two pounds and was used to protect the head from bullets and shrapnel. It was made of a two-piece combination of steel and fiberglass, and could serve as a washbasin, a cooking pot or a bowl.

The wool uniform had the greatest functionality, keeping the soldiers warm in the cold winter weather. The combat boots had a permanently attached two-buckled leather ankle flap, rubberized tops and soles and were worn with wool ski socks. While the boots were effective in keeping feet from soaking and freezing, they lacked foot support and wore out quickly, resulting in foot injuries when the soldiers marched in the freezing weather. When the soldiers stopped to rest, the perspiration-soaked socks froze, and so did their feet inside the boots.

The men in Sandy's unit, Sandy included, were frightened newcomers, mostly teenagers, fresh from civilian life. These young recruits, replacing the thousands of men who were killed or taken prisoner during the Battle of the Bulge just a month ago, experienced on-the-job training in a hostile and chaotic environment and were often unable to grapple with the danger. Still, each soldier acted as if he knew exactly what to do. Tragically, many errors resulted from the naïveté of inexperience, and injuries and deaths occurred. Blunders were common, and comfort came only from knowing that the enemy made mistakes, too.

Beth thought the men looked like nervous high school students, doomed teenagers who were woefully unprepared for the horrors that lay ahead. They were shunned by many of the veteran combat troops who knew from bitter experience that new replacements didn't last long. And they had little training on how to deal with the psychological trauma of combat. One new soldier didn't know how to use his

M1 rifle so a more experienced soldier showed him. He then fired only one shot, the one that killed himself.

Sandy and the Infantry troops stayed near Marseille until mid-February, struggling with an intense training schedule. In addition to infantry-tank training, there was instruction in mine and booby trap setting, and lectures on the handling of captured enemy documents and prisoners of war. And all weapons were tested at a nearby firing range. Regular hours, showers, and meals helped restore the morale of the men who had been in Europe with the Rainbow since the Battle of the Bulge and had witnessed the deaths of so many of their buddies. The new guys listened to the stories of the seasoned soldiers as they prepared for their encounters. One of the things they heard repeatedly was that German sympathizers were everywhere and no one, not even children, could be trusted.

Each soldier had a particular job while waiting for orders to move to the front. Sandy's job was guard duty, so he spent the freezing evenings walking the perimeter of the large camp. Beth, unamused and way too cold, stayed snuggled up on Sandy's cot in his tent, under his pillow and wool blanket. Sandy might have guard duty but Beth sure as hell didn't!

January 25, 1945
My Dearest Darling Wife:
I just got through walking guard duty and thought I'd write to you now because it's still kind of early and it's the only chance I've had today. It's about eight-thirty here now and it's five hours later than it is at home. I keep wondering what you are doing at different times. I suppose now you are just finishing work and are going over to the store.

I'm writing from my tent. I have a candle fixed here and it serves two purposes, light and heat. Not so much for heat but it does throw off a little light.

Walking guard duty here is a lot different than it was in the States. Here we use live ammunition.

Today is the hardest I've worked since I got here and I almost finished my job today so I'll have it considerably easier tomorrow.

It's been a beautiful evening, Darling. The moon here has been out all evening and it's so bright and beautiful that it looks like daytime, and it makes the mind wander thousands of miles away, although my mind hasn't really even been over here. It's been with you all the time, Darling.

I have to go on guard duty at twelve-thirty, Darling, so I guess I'll close for tonight and get a little sleep before I go back on. So until tomorrow, Darling, I close loving you with all my heart.

Your loving hubby,
Sandy

The men who had been doing guard duty received a welcomed surprise when they awoke the next day. They were being sent to Paris for a day of relaxation and whatever else soldiers do when they're in a beautiful city with beautiful women. Beth and Sandy were very excited to go into a town, any town really, thinking they'd get real food and decent coffee. They didn't, of course, because there was none. Paris had already seen its share of fighting though it wasn't nearly as destroyed as the towns they would soon encounter. But it was left without electricity, little food, and no way to heat the buildings that remained.

Ketch and the other guys were excited to see the women. They offered them chocolate bars, hard candies, chewing gum, and cigarettes in exchange for sex. Beth tried to ignore their disgusting sexist chatter. Sandy kept his wife's photo at the center of his focus. It was a challenge for him, especially getting teased by his buddies for not "partaking of the goods," but Sandy was committed. He took a break from walking to write to Lois. Beth suspected it might be out of the guilt he felt from the less-than-honorable thoughts he probably held after being teased by Ketch.

January 26, 1945
My Dearest Darling Wife:

At present I am in a city in France. We got a pass today so we came in. It was a beautiful city before the war, I guess, but it has been greatly ruined. Some of the sights are really worth seeing. They have small street cars pulling trailers and the people just run up and down the street and jump on them. They ride on top, hang on the sides and anywhere that there is an inch of room. This is a pretty modern place, though, I guess. They have those trolley busses here.

It seems so funny when you go to buy something, you can't carry on a conversation with them because they just know French. We carry a book with us and we can tell them what we want, but when they talk back to us, that's where we cave in. It's really a lot of fun, though.

Money has no value here. You go into a store and buy something and the prices they ask are incredible. You can't buy anything to eat in the restaurants and all of the buildings are cold. You can't imagine what it's like over here in this war-torn country, Darling, and I hope you'll never know. That's why I'm here.

Beth wondered if Sandy was beginning to figure out why he was there?

I wish you could be here with me, Darling. I think that I could be a much better soldier if I had you with me all the time. In fact, I'm sure of it.

I just hate to close a letter when I write to you, Darling, because when I'm writing to you, it's almost the same as if I was talking to you. But right now I'm practically speechless. So I'll close with loads and loads of love and kisses and reminding you, Darling, that I love you more than words can express.

Your loving hubby,
Sandy

"Dude, really???" Beth was incredulous. "You wish she were here with you? This is about the most romantic place ever...NOT!"

"Nah," Sandy replied. "Not really. I just wish she and I were together, somewhere, anywhere. It's tough being in town and watching the other guys pick up girls. It's too easy. The girls are everywhere and willing to have sex with anyone."

"I know, Pop," said, Beth, a little less harshly. She was beginning to feel sorry for him. "I saw those women come on to you but you held your ground. And I know it was difficult. Most of these guys are married, just like you, but that didn't stop them. Aren't they scared of getting some disease? Didn't they hear those sex lectures we had to sit through?"

"The fellas don't care about that, Beth."

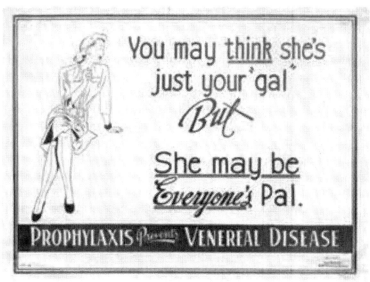

U.S. Army WWII training poster

Then after thinking for a moment, Sandy asked, "Do you think those girls are just looking for American husbands to take them back to the States?"

"Sure," responded Beth. "I bet some are, but mostly, I suspect it's all about survival for them. They're in a war-torn town with little food and money and resources. You guys come in with your few bucks and some candy bars and cigarettes, and the girls are in business! That part doesn't bother me as much as the other thing that I saw." Beth drifted for a moment.

"What was that?" asked Sandy, a bit curious though he really had little concern for the locals.

"Well," Beth hesitated, "Some of the men were rough with the women, treating them like shit – sorry... I mean, like pieces of dirt. There was a sense of cruelty about those guys, like they were saying, 'I'm American and powerful and I'm just taking you, like it or not.'"

"Aw, they don't mean anything by it, Beth. They're just lonely and on edge. We all are. We know the jerries are right around the corner but we've not had a chance to fight them yet. We're all tense."

"That's true, Pop, but it's no reason to treat women badly, to use or even abuse them."

"They're not abusing them. Those girls like it."

"What? What makes you say something like that? Of *course* they don't like it! Why would they? Because you guys are such great catches??? I DOUBT it!"

Now Beth was stumped. How could Sandy say something like that? Did he, and the other guys, really believe that the women *like* being treated poorly by men who can't speak their language, who think they're objects and not people? Really????

January 28, 1945
My Dearest Darling Wife:

I don't know how much time I'll have to write now. It's been raining and that has caused a little slowness in the start of our work. It's so damn cold and I hated the walk to the Red Cross tent. It's almost too cold to write but my heart got the best of me, Darling, so I just want to write to you now.

Guess what, Darling? I just got some mail, the first since I left the States and although it was almost four weeks old, you'd be surprised how good that made me feel. But the worst part was there wasn't any from you, Darling. The airmail hasn't arrived yet. I hope to get some from you soon.

I have to close now, Darling, so until later I remain
Your loving hubby
Sandy

These young soldiers were someone's son, brother, husband, lover, friend. They were terribly frightened but they anchored themselves by bravery and commitment. First and foremost they were Americans. Citizen soldiers. They were ordinary Americans who confronted the best that enemy forces could throw at them, and they emerged victorious at nearly every turn. Except Sandy's unit had yet to see battle. They marched and moved forward through thick dark forests and bombed-out towns, through severe cold and snow, to get to the front.

To keep from feeling the fear and anticipation too much, the troops were entertained in a variety of ways. There were newly-released movies shown on portable screens, and USO—United Service Organization—shows where celebrities brought their bands and productions to the battlefront. The Red Cross Clubmobile units provided a touch of home by having American coffee and doughnuts served by American women.

The Rest Centers in Nancy, France and Luxembourg were the favorites for the soldiers, offering hot meals and hot showers. The men would go for weeks in the freezing cold without showers, so the Rest Centers were special for them. The Centers were also places where the men could have some time and paper and pencils to write letters home.

January 29, 1945
My Dearest Darling Wife:
I got two of the most wonderful letters and the most beautiful Valentine that I have ever seen, and you can't imagine how they made me feel, Darling.

I'm sorry that I couldn't write yesterday, Darling, but I was on guard duty and when I was off, my candle had ended when I wrote a letter to mom, so I couldn't write. Tonight I'm sitting by a fire and writing to you. This isn't the best way to write but I just couldn't go another evening without writing to you.

I want to thank you ever so much for the lovely thoughtful Valentine, Darling. It was beautiful but it made me feel so bad because I know you'll think that I'm neglecting you because I haven't sent you any, but believe me, Darling, if I could get something or a Valentine to send to you, I would, regardless of the price, but I just can't get anything here. You are my Valentine and I love you very much and I'll try to make it up to you later on.

I have to sign off for tonight, Darling because the fire is dying down and I must get my sleep. So until tomorrow, Darling, I remain
    Your loving hubby
    Sandy

Beth realized that though Valentine's Day was still a couple of weeks away, Lois and the folks back home had to send items early for a timely arrival. She decided not to harass Sandy about it.

———————————

New sleeping bags arrived for the front-line infantry, and liquor rations came for the officers. It was extremely cold, and the soldiers wore every piece of clothing they could get their hands on. The overcoats were quite warm but when they got wet and muddy they became very heavy. Gloves were quickly lost, so soldiers put socks on their hands to ward off the cold. They were issued new combat boots, but when the boots got wet, the soldiers often got trench foot and frostbite. They learned quickly not to lace their boots too tight because it constricted blood flow. In addition, the Recon men also carried binoculars around their necks and a portable radio on their backs.

January 30, 1945
My Dearest Darling Wife:
  I hope we hurry up and kick those Nazis, which I hope won't take too long. I'm writing this letter to you from my pup tent. We're living like soldiers now, or in other words, like dogs. Our food has improved quite a bit today from what it's been, though, and you'd be surprised how much it does for a soldier's morale to get good food.

Beth commented, "Dude, the food sucks!
"It's not so bad," said Sandy.
"You must have a very nondiscriminating palate!"
"Huh?"
"Never mind. Keep writing."

  It's pretty cold here but after you're out for a while and you can't go into a warm place, it just becomes unnoticeable.
  Today should be Leon's bar mitzvah. I wish I could have been there for my only brother's celebration. I know he does, too. But I guess it just has to be this way. How did he do?
  We turned in our money today to be exchanged for francs. We're only permitted to keep one dollar in American currency and the

rest all has to be changed. It'll seem awfully funny to use francs after using dollars and cents all my life.

I'll continue writing now. We were interrupted long enough to take a hike and it's raining. There's nothing like taking a hike in the rain and mud.

I guess this is enough to write for one day, Darling. I'll try to write some more tomorrow. So until then, I'll close loving you with all my heart. I remain

Your loving hubby
Sandy

By January 1945, thousands of soldiers in the 42nd Rainbow Division had been killed, and thousands more had just arrived from the U.S. to replace them. Sandy was one of those replacements. They landed in Marseille, set up camps several miles away from the landing site and awaited orders. The first orders included training for the new replacement troops since they had yet to experience battle. While they had trained back in the States, they had not killed others nor seen their buddies die. Battle was bad enough. It became exceptionally perilous with combat rookies. Commanding General Harold Linden sent a letter to each of the soldiers who had been on the battlefield for several months as well as to the new replacements:

31 January 1945
To the Officers and Men of the Rainbow Infantry Regiments:
You men of the 42d Infantry Division and our gallant comrades who fell on the battlefield have just written Chapter 1 of Volume II of the history of the Rainbow.

By your courage and ability you have demonstrated that the Infantry of the Rainbow Division of World War II is a tough, hard-hitting team, capable of destroying the enemy any place and any time it meets him.

Your baptism of fire was fast and furious; and received in carrying out the mission of holding an important Seventh Army sector against experienced German troops intent on regaining Alsace. You fought the powerful 10th and 21st Panzer Divisions and you and the troops who fought with you prevented these units from reaching their objective.

At Gambsheim, Hatten and Sessenheim you showed that you have what it takes to meet the German and destroy him. At Schweighausen and Kaltenhouse you repulsed strong German attacks, as a result of which the enemy drive was stopped cold on the Haguenau positions with approximately 1,100 Germans dead. His effort to retake Alsace was a failure.

No single effort of an individual or an organization need be singled out to illustrate your courage and your strength. Everyone had a job to do, and everyone did it to the best of his ability. For this I am proud of all of you.

Now we are in a period of training. Your experiences against the enemy should prove to you that you cannot win with courage alone. You must have skill. You must know everything there is to know about your job, and you can never know too much.

The tricks that you learned in combat – and you learned many of them – must be taught to your new comrades, for it is they who will revitalize your squads and platoons. Welcome these men into your organization. Together you will write Chapter 2 of Volume II of the history of the Rainbow.

You and your new comrades must prepare in this short training period to drive again toward Berlin and the destruction of the German army. Mistakes in war cost human lives. Profit by the mistakes that you made in your first engagements. TRAIN, TRAIN, and TRAIN that the same mistakes shall not re-occur.

This is the period in which you can take out life insurance. Make every minute of it count.

HENNING LINDEN
Brigadier General, U.S. Army
Commanding

Beth again wondered, *Why do they do it? What makes these young soldiers perform in the face of tremendous fear, loneliness, and danger?*

Some American soldiers wanted to fight against totalitarianism, and the murder of civilians. But most described a far less sense of purpose. War veteran and historian Paul Fussell reflected, "To get home you had to end the war. To end the war was the reason you fought it. The only reason." Many of the soldiers did not fight for battlefield glory or patriotic sacrifice. They were simply driven by the desire to get back home to a normal life with family and friends.

Beth thought, *It has to be more than just wanting to get home. What is it?*

7.

SANDY'S STORY

The fighting had not yet begun which was frustrating for the replacement troops who were itching to see action. But they were inexperienced and training was still a necessary daily event. After one particularly hard day of practice with rifles, Sandy and his buddies settled in for the evening. Dinner had already been served and the day was dark, the sun setting early in the cold, cloudy horizon. As the sun went down, so did the temperature. It was freezing.

Sandy and Beth were quiet, trying to stay warm. Sandy was shaking. Beth wondered if it was from the cold or from the fear that each of the men in Sandy's unit felt. To make conversation, Beth asked, "Pop, what's it like to be you? To be a kid from God-knows-where East Liverpool, Ohio, wherever *that* is. I don't know anything about you or your family." Beth knew the conversation might help Sandy think about something other than his fear. "So, you and Lois knew one another as little kids, right?"

"Right."

"Were you in the same grades in school together?"

"We were, though Lois is a year younger than I. She'd skipped a grade when she was in elementary school because she's so smart. We graduated from East Liverpool High School, in June, 1943. I had just turned 18 and Lois had just turned 17. That was less than two years ago but it seems like a lifetime has passed..." Sandy faded off.

"Pop, what was your family of origin like?" Beth brought him back to the present.

"Huh? Uh, my what??? What's a family of origin?"

"You know, like, your parents and stuff."

"Oh. I get it. Sure. I'm really dedicated to my parents. I always worked for them in their store, and took care of my younger sisters and brother, especially since my brother was always getting into trouble of some sort. I think I started in my dad's store when I was four years old! All we had was immediate family because so many others were killed in Poland. Those who didn't die or escape during WWI were killed just a few years ago by the Nazis." He thought for a moment then continued. "I think that's one of the reasons why I liked Lois so much from the start. She has relatives, family, and I always felt like one of them.

But my dad runs the show. He's respected by everyone in town even though he speaks with an accent. He mostly speaks Polish or Yiddish.

"Yiddish? What's Yiddish?" Beth didn't know.

"Hmmm...Yiddish is kind of a combination of German and Hebrew, I think. Kind of a secret language for Jews." Sandy became thoughtful. "My dad is the most respected man in our town, I'm sure. I want to be respected like that, too, one day."

"East Liverpool," said Beth. "Funny name. Sounds like someplace the Beatles should be from."

"The who?"

"The Beatles. Oh, right. Forget it. It's 1945. No Beatles yet. That's kind of funny though. The Beatles are still just babies!" She chuckled about that momentarily. Then, more seriously, she asked," What's East Liverpool like? I live in St. Petersburg, Florida, and it's kind of crowded, too much traffic, too many people. Is East Liverpool like that?"

"Nah. East Liverpool... it's such a small town. Everyone knows everybody else, knows everybody's business. A kid can't get away with anything because the neighbor down the street might be the one to spank him as readily as his own parents would. My family lives in the East End on Thompson Avenue in a three-story house. We have a store on Bradshaw and Ambrose. Lois' family lives downtown, at 310 West 5th. Her mother, who I really love, is probably the reason Lois and I got married. She's very ill, her mother. Colitis something. I don't really know what that is."

"You said your parents came to the U.S. from Poland? When did they get there, Pop?"

"Good question. I think my mother came to the U.S. from Kurow, Poland in about 1908. Her name is Pauline Pearl Feldberg Lebman. Her family sent her. We always thought she was an orphan. I'm not sure now, and she never talks about her family. But I do know that when she got to the U.S., she had to go through Ellis Island in New York. She was met there by her two older sisters, Gussie and Lillie Feldberg. They lived at 130 Attorney Street in the Lower East Side of Manhattan, New York, and worked in the garment district."

Beth said, "My mom is an historian so she did a lot of research about our families. What you're saying seems to be accurate with what I've heard from her. She also says that your mother Pauline is in the 1910 and 1930 census but not the 1920 census. Why do you think that is?"

"Damned if I know. I don't even know what that means! Do you know anything about my father? He's even more of a mystery because no one asks so he doesn't say anything."

"I know some stuff, Pop, though it might be best if you just ask him."

"Ask him? I don't have that kind of family, Beth. We're close and all but we just don't talk about anything personal. What do you know...and how do you know it?"

"Like I said, my mom, your granddaughter, is an historian and she's been digging into your family for a long time. It seems your dad came to the U.S. as a stowaway on a ship. He and some other dude. They were being chased by the Russian army or something, I don't know, because of their work in the Polish resistance. He came to the U.S. in 1913." Sandy listened to this young woman who seemed to know much more than he about his own family.

"Your dad and his friend were stowaways on a ship from France to New York. Because your dad was a stowaway, he didn't have papers to enter the U.S., and wasn't sponsored by anyone like your mom was, which was a requirement, so he couldn't go through Ellis Island like your mom did. When his ship entered New York harbor, he and the other dude jumped overboard and swam to Battery Park. Pretty cool, really! My great-great-grandfather as an undocumented immigrant!"

"A what?" asked Sandy. It didn't sound so good to him.

"Never mind," said Beth, knowing that was a go-nowhere conversation. "He apparently knew your mom from Poland and knew where to find her."

Beth paused, took a drink of water and continued, "Your dad got a job in a grocery store and saved enough money to buy his own grocery cart. His name was Saul Ruchelsman but the grocery cart was called Lebman's. Your dad had just enough money to buy the cart but not enough to repaint and change the name, so he took on the name on the cart as his own. He became Saul Lebman and peddled groceries on the Lower East Side where your mom lived."

Sandy was fascinated. "Did they get married there?"

"No, it doesn't appear so. Your mom was still pretty young. She and her sisters worked in a clothing factory with other Jewish and Italian immigrant women and girls. Your mom's sisters probably died in the Spanish flu epidemic when it hit New York, around 1917. Your mom was sent to Cleveland, probably by her sisters before they died, where people from her town in Poland lived. Your dad must have followed her there. They moved together to East Liverpool by 1923 because your oldest sister Esther was born there that year. They may have gone to East Liverpool because it felt similar to the *shtetl*, the little village, they left in Poland, and it had two synagogues which was important to your parents."

"So is that where they were married?"

"Good question. Not sure. Based on what my mom found, it's unlikely they were legally married at all because your dad was an undocumented immigrant, not an American citizen. They eventually got married in the synagogue while…this is so weird…while you were in training at Camp Gruber last fall. Your brother was the best man."

"Yeah, I know they had something in the synagogue recently. I wondered why they did that, and why then?"

"If you want to know, Pop, ask them," said Beth, knowing that he never will.

Beth asked another question. "How did you end up in the Recons, Pop? You *know* we're gonna be out in front, right? I'm not looking forward to that too much."

"I don't know. Like everything else, it seems, it just happened. I wanted to be a pharmacist and was enrolled at Ohio State University to begin my program of study in the fall of 1943. While I really did want to avenge the deaths of my family in Poland, I also wanted to go to school. Even my parents didn't want me to enlist. But the decision wasn't mine. I got drafted and placed in the Recons. Nobody asked me what I'd prefer. I don't know if I'll make it to college later on."

No way I'm gonna tell him he doesn't, thought Beth. Some things are best left unsaid.

"Okay, I have another question for you. Why did you get married so young?"

"What young? Everybody gets married right out of high school. We actually waited a year after graduation. We were the old couple!" Sandy chuckled. "But we got married because I was in love with Lois, and with me being in the army and all, we thought it was the right thing to do."

Sandy continued, "In the fall of 1943, I was injured at basic training. Some idiot pulled the pin on his grenade in our training pit. Stupid jerk! I threw my helmet down on the grenade then fell on it. It exploded and I got blown to smithereens! Shrapnel all over my body from it. So they sent me home on a medical furlough. By then I was promoted from Private to Private First Class."

"That's a promotion? Dude, I hate to tell you but PFC isn't that high up on the military food chain."

"True, but it beats being a buck private, the lowest of the low, and the pay was a bit better."

"The medical furlough. What happened then?" Beth was attentive and wanted to know more.

"I went home but I didn't tell Lois I was coming. I knew she'd been baking cookies for other soldiers but not for me. I wasn't too happy about that. I'm kind of the jealous type. Her mother invited me to dinner the night I returned. Lois was surprised to see me but seemed happy about it. We dated every night of my furlough. I wanted to elope but Lois said she was too young. Even though she had graduated from high school already, she was still just 17."

Sandy continued with his story: They'd known each other since elementary school. Sandy Lebman and Lois Schonfield were friends, having met when his father and her mother volunteered at the small synagogue in East Liverpool. Sandy was painfully shy on one hand, and overly obsessive about the well-being of his immediate family on the other. Being the oldest son, he took serious responsibility for his sisters and brother. He had worked for his father his entire young life, in the family grocery store or the family hardware store, whichever the resourceful Saul Lebman was operating at the time.

Sandy didn't date much in high school. He was in love with Lois from a very young age. One day when they were still quite young, 13-year old Sandy was walking west on East 5th Street as Lois and Sandy's sister Fran were walking east. Sandy hollered across the street to her, "Some day I'm going to marry you, Lois!" She hollered back, "Shut up!"

"But I knew I would marry her," laughed Sandy.

He continued. "I was pretty shy as a kid and Lois was so beautiful, so popular. But I knew I was going to marry her. I just needed for her to know that, too. Her parents ran the S&S Shoe Store in town but because her mother was always so ill, they had very little money. I was so quiet around her, well, around most girls. I wasn't confident, but Lois's mother really loved me and made me feel kind of important, so I was always able to at least get a foot in their door. For Lois's birthday every year, I'd get her a little gift so she'd go out with me, and she usually did for a couple of months. Then nothing. My damned shyness

68

always kept me from talking, kept me from engaging in anything with her."

Beth interrupted. "Is that when you got married then? While you were home on that furlough?"

"Nah. I did ask Lois to marry me, like I said before. Well, I asked her to elope. She said no to eloping but she did say yes to marrying me. I was excited and wanted to give her a ring, so my dad and I went to Jim Reese's jewelry store. Mr. Reese gave me a dozen rings and said, 'Take these to Lois and see which she likes, then bring the rest back.' Lois worked in the bank at the time, so I took the rings to her there and put them on her counter. Once she got over the surprise, she selected a very beautiful ring. I took the others back to the jewelry store. My father paid for the ring. We got married last April. April 16th. Our first anniversary is in a couple of months. I doubt I'll get to be with her to celebrate."

Yeah, you won't see her for another year, thought Beth, but again she didn't have the heart to tell him.

"Did Lois go back to the army base with you after you got married?"

"Lois came with me back to Camp Gruber where we lived for a few months then we went to Fort Riley, Kansas. She came with me to Ft. Riley and found a job there. We lived in a small box of an apartment. Several months later I was ordered back to Camp Gruber because we were going to be shipping out soon. Lois and I were able to ride the train together to St. Louis, then Lois transferred to East Liverpool to be with our families. I kept going on to Oklahoma. While there I received extended training in the cavalry, which means I learned to ride a horse, and I was also trained as a radioman. I was assigned to this Reconnaissance unit as part of the 42nd Rainbow Division....funny, that was just a couple of months ago. Seems like years."

Sandy had been assigned to the Reconnaissance unit of the 42nd Rainbow Division, company 222G, at Camp Gruber. There were only ninety Recons in the entire division. Recons were in a select situation in that they were always out in front, usually in M8 armored cars, sometimes on horses. Sandy knew his job was to reconnoiter at the front lines, decide what was needed, which troops to send and how many, then radio back to the Command Post. But the guns...

"The biggest problem I have is that I'm supposed to fire a gun. I'd never handled a gun, any gun, and now I'm looking at a heavy machine gun...and all kinds of ammunition. Everyone had to learn to aim to see how good we were. Man, it's so hard on the ears. Very noisy. I don't know how you're gonna handle it, Beth. Did you bring ear plugs?"

"Don't worry about me, Dude. I'm Beth America! I'm prepared." She took earplugs out of her pocket to show him.

"The biggest problem, I think," said Sandy, "is that I've never shot at anything or anyone before. And now I have to kill people. But I'm okay with that because the Nazis killed my family. I need to get them back."

Sandy told Beth about the trip from Oklahoma to New York as his unit prepared to go overseas. "It was three days in a big long troop train. It stopped in dinky towns where we had to get off the train and run a mile or so, do exercises, then get back on the train. The food was crap. Oh, sorry, Beth. The food stunk. But civilians came out to watch and cheer us on. They knew we were going to war. It felt good to hear their cheers. We finally got to Camp Kilmer in New Jersey and did last-minute things like get shots, make out wills, get religion. A lot of the guys went into New York City for some fun."

"Did you go, too, Pop? You, uh, seem like a not-fun, way-too-serious kind of guy."

"Hey! I can be a fun guy! Yeah, I did. I went, too," he said proudly. "My buddy Ketchum over there and Dickie Wilson and AJ Jackson and I went. You met those guys, or rather, you've seen them." Sandy thought it best not to mention Beth to his pals, or to anyone for that matter. He took a deep breath and made a long sigh...

"So here I sit, half way 'round the world, talking to my imagination. I'm losing it and we haven't even begun to fight."

"I'm not your imagination, Pop. Get over it! I'm really, just, well, different. And since I'm your great granddaughter, I need for you to live through this mess so I can be born!"

Sandy looked at her, maybe for the first time. "When are you, uh, born?"

"1995."

"And who's your mother again?"

"Your granddaughter, Berit."

"And who's *her* mother?"

"Your oldest child, your daughter, Ronni."

"I'm so confused."

"No worries, Dude. It'll make sense one day."

8.

FEBRUARY, 1945:

THE MOVEMENT FORWARD BEGINS

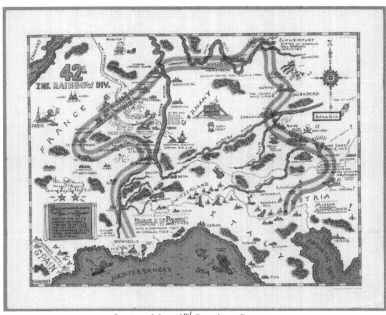

*Route of the 42nd Rainbow Division
Europe, January-May 1945*

Sandy, Ketch, AJ, Dickie, and the men from their unit went back to Paris on January 31st. Though Paris had been liberated from the Germans only eight months earlier, fighting throughout France continued. But for today, Paris again welcomed the young American soldiers. They had become enthralled with the Eiffel Tower, the pastries, the Avenue des Champs-Élysées, and the Arc de Triomphe. Sandy and Beth spent much of the time wandering the streets of Paris, marveling at its beauty and its history. The other men had disappeared to the areas where women called to them.

Women of every age and marital status openly solicited for sex. Parks, bombed-out buildings, cemeteries, railway tracks, even the banks of the River Seine were places where women worked. Women supported themselves and their families by means of prostitution. Little children and old men solicited on every street for their sisters, mothers or daughters, then escorted soldiers to their homes. Soldiers quickly learned such phrases in French as *I am not married* and *Are your parents home?*

At one point, a Paris official suggested the Americans set up a brothel outside the city to avoid public outrage and to contain the spread of sexually transmitted diseases. The Americans declined, and U.S. officers publicly denounced the behavior, but they did little to curtail it. The U.S. Army actually did eventually set up brothels in both France and Italy, complete with daily medical inspections of women to keep the sexually transmitted disease rates low. In Paris, the French military also set up brothels. Long lines of soldiers formed outside.

Sex was not always consensual, and thousands of cases of rape were reported to authorities: 3,500 rapes by American soldiers in France were reported between June 1944 and May 1945. In fact, American soldiers in Europe raped over 14,000 civilian women in England, France and Germany. Some of the men were punished for sexual violence, and 70 American soldiers were executed. Other Allied soldiers were no better, and the Russian soldiers were brutal, using rape as a weapon of war.

But on this day, the American soldiers, many away from home for the first time, were out on the town in Paris.

"Hey, Sandy! Coming with us? Dames are everywhere! They want us! And they're cheap!" Ketch and the others headed toward the red-light district. The men were young, had money in their pockets, and were tremendously horny.

"Nah...you go on. I'm married and intend to stay true to my wife."

"I'm married, too," said Dickie Wilson but we're a million miles from home and we might not make it back."

"That's okay, fellas. I'm going to see as much as I can of Paris."

Beth was impressed. "Pop, I won't tell anyone. Go ahead. Don't not play because I'm here. I have plenty of other things to do."

Sandy laughed. "Now *this* is a strange conversation to have with my so-called great-granddaughter!" He became thoughtful. "It's just that I don't want anyone else. And I don't know if I'll ever get back to Paris again." *You don't*, thought Beth. "Great idea," she said.

Soldiers with a prostitute, Paris

Back at camp, USO shows helped soldiers forget they were in the middle of war. The Army didn't want the soldiers to feel anything, just do their jobs of killing the enemy. USO shows served as tremendous distractions for fear and homesickness. The Bob Hope show was internationally famous, and the Andrews Sisters, Bing Crosby, and many others brought fun and levity to the battlefront. There were also plenty of first-run movies and a large selection of books. Sandy enjoyed all of it.

The men devised other diversions as well. Gambling was a favorite, betting on everything from rats to snowflakes. Sandy learned cribbage, a game he continued to play back home until his death in 2013.

Feb. 10, 1945
My Dearest Darling Wife:
Well, I guess I can let you in on a little military status, as to where and what I'm doing now.

"It's about damned time!" interrupted Beth.

I am, as you might have heard on the radio or read in the newspaper, in the Seventh Army, and I haven't as yet seen any combat. I don't know exactly just when we will see it but I have a pretty darned good idea.

"No kidding. Those planes are getting awfully close!" exclaimed Beth. Sandy nodded slightly in agreement but ignored her as he continued to write.

Coming across France we saw many German vehicles and weapons that had been knocked out and abandoned in the chase, and when you hear that the Germans were beaten in France, it's no exaggeration. They really took a beating but they're in Germany now and they're tough and I doubt very much if they'll be knocked out as fast as some people think they will be, although this war can't end fast enough to suit me.

"Or me…"

I guess I shouldn't talk about military situations to you, Darling, because you're probably not interested but we haven't been permitted to write some of that for security sake and when they did permit us to write it, I thought I'd take advantage of it. I hope I haven't bored you too much, Darling.
Well, I must take a sponge bath now. That's the only kind we can take here but they certainly make you feel better.
So until next time, my darling, I close loving you always very dearly.
Your loving hubby,
Sandy

"Pop, why would you think she's not interested? Her husband is here, her country's at war, and you write about taking a bath! Of COURSE she's interested! She's not stupid! Sheeeesh! I need to go see her."

"How can you go see her?"

"How did I get here, Dude? I can go anywhere I want."

"Would you come back?" Sandy had become attached to his annoying little whatever-she-is.

"That's a good one! You think I'm a figment of your imagination yet you invite me back to this, uh, paradise. Hell, yeah, I'll come back. I need to see for myself how this thing ends. There's still so much I need to know. But I'm not going yet so don't cry for me, Argentina."

"Huh?"

"Sorry, Dude. Just a saying from a movie…."

Sandy's letter seemed shallow to Beth. "You know, if I were your wife, I'd think you were somewhere on business, not in a friggin' war!"

"I can't write about what's really going on here! I told you! It would just get censored. So all I can do is write what I feel in the few minutes that I have. I don't even know if she'll get any of these, or if I'll still be alive when she does."

"Dude! Don't you pay attention? If you didn't live, I wouldn't be here now!"

Thoughtfully Sandy said, "Things are so messed up over here, I'm not sure you're real, so that doesn't even make sense to me."

———————

It was more than a month before the Rainbow replacement troops engaged in their first combat after landing in Marseilles. Everyone was fearful, but there was much work to be done. On February 14th, the Rainbow as a whole entered combat, taking up defensive positions near Hagenau in the Hardt Forest. After a month of extensive training, patrolling and active defense, the Rainbow went on the offensive.

Feb. 14, 1945
My Dearest Darling Valentine:

Is that name appropriate for the date, Darling? I've been thinking all day what you would be thinking of me not sending you a Valentine as lovely as those that you sent me. I'm very hurt that I couldn't send you one but I can send you all my love, Darling. That's about all I can do.

I've got about five pictures of you here, Darling, and that's not enough to fit all around the inside of my turret. The number of my car is Lucky Thirteen, Darling. That number always seemed to bring me luck before and here's hoping it comes through again. Don't forget to take a drink to good ole' thirteen.

I'm sitting here again tonight writing to the one I love by the light of the campfire. I'm getting so used to writing by a fire that I hardly know what it's like to have a light. But a campfire seems to make things more romantic, don't you think so, Darling? You ought to try it sometime.

"Oh, brother! You are totally sappy!" Beth didn't hold back the sarcasm though she had developed a quiet but unspoken admiration for Sandy's romanticism.

"Quit reading over my shoulder!" Sandy was only mildly annoyed. He kept writing.

You know, Darling, I've been trying to keep all your letters but they've been accumulating pretty rapidly and space is very limited. In fact, we haven't enough room for our necessities so I've been forced to burn some, and you don't know how it hurts me to burn your letters. I hope you don't mind too much.

I'll close sending you all my love and kisses and remaining yours always,
Your loving hubby,
Sandy

The weather was now horrific with drenching rain and freezing cold, which made movement all the more difficult. They were on the front lines near Wimmenau in the Hardt mountains northwest of Hagenau. Despite being caked in mud and ice, the men marched on.

Feb. 16, 1945
My Very Dearest Darling Wife:

Well, here I am writing again after that brief lapse of time although it seems as though it has been ages since I last wrote to you. You see, Darling, we've been on the go for a few days now, and I didn't have a chance at all to write although I wanted to very badly. The weather has been miserable which handicapped my writing to you. I've seen quite a bit of France now. I can feel fine in saying that when you hear or read that France has been hit hard, don't doubt it in the least because they have been. They haven't got any food, fuel, or clothing.

The people here, Darling, are wearing wooden shoes, just like those you see pictures of Hollanders wear. They have a felt slipper that fits inside of the shoe, and whenever they enter a house, they take the wooden shoes off and wear the slippers in the house.

We went through some cities and they were already very bombed out, burnt clear to the ground. You can't begin to imagine what it's like until you see it yourself.

At present, Darling, I am billeting in a French village. My address is 27 Rue du Mont. Naturally you won't use that address. I just thought I'd tell you. It's a farming village and almost every house is either above a barn or connected to it in some way. There are six of us staying in one room here. We've got it arranged pretty nicely considering we haven't got any beds or anything, and in the morning when we wake up and open our shutters, there's the biggest, most handsome pile of manure out there and, man, what an aroma! Just like evening in Paris or more like morning in Calcutta.

I'm glad to hear that you have been ice skating and having a good time because at least one of us can have a good time. I haven't skated much this year, just a little in Tulsa.

I'm terribly sorry to hear about Grandma having to have her leg amputated, Darling. When you see her again, tell her I said hello.

It's dark now, Darling, and since there is no electric here right now due to a slight bombing near here yesterday, we rigged up a light.

"Slight?? Are you kidding??? It was scary as hell!"

I'm glad you're taking over my job as bookkeeper for Dad, darling. I'd rather see you do it than anyone else. It makes me feel good to know that my wife is taking care of my job while I'm away.

Isn't it funny, I no sooner get over seas and I get a letter from you that Dave Silverberg has been coming around again. It seems as though every time I get a good distance from you, he always shows up. Doesn't look so good, does it, Darling?

"Dude, are you the jealous type? I seriously hadn't figured you for that!" Sandy ignored her.

The next time you see him, tell him I'm sorry and I won't marry his type any more. He can have all the rest of them.

The people in this village are very nice, Darling. They'd do anything in this world for us. I think that they're afraid that we might treat them the same way the Germans did. Anyhow, regardless of what it is, they just can't seem to do enough for us.

I sure would like to be home with you now, Darling. I never knew it would be so hard being without you as it is now. Your picture is always in front of me regardless of where I am or what I'm doing. Right now it is adorning my room and you'd be surprised how bright it makes it.

I have to close for now, Darling, so until tomorrow I'll close remaining only yours.

Your loving hubby,
Sandy

———————————

It was finally time to fight the Nazis. Combat began at midnight on February 17. Sandy and the Recons began patrolling to determine enemy strength. The men on the front line dug foxholes. The rest were billeted in French homes or buildings that had been evacuated and taken over by the troops.

The German army was well prepared and had laid thousands of mines along the front. Most of the mines were small and intended for use against individual soldiers, set off by a man's weight. The explosion would destroy a foot and the lower part of a leg. The Rainbow Division, in exchange, set up booby-traps and tripwires to ensnare enemy patrols.

The Infantry started the attack. Loaded with bazookas and ammunition, the Rainbow soldiers moved forward. They directed mortar fire at enemy installations throughout the day and night. Counterattack plans were coordinated with all supporting troops. Active patrolling was used to harass the enemy and to insure continuous contact with them.

The winter was the coldest in 25 years as the troops moved into the front. Many Rainbow men were lost earlier in December and January during the Battle of the Bulge. The new young replacement soldiers like Sandy had no idea what the immediate future held nor how horrible it would be. They knew only that they were there to do a job and hopefully go home in one piece.

February 19,1945
My Dearest Darling Wife:
   Believe it or not I am on my first mission and writing to you, so you see, even in combat, I find some time to write.
   I've got it pretty soft. All I do is sit down here by a radio with a telephone in one hand and a key in the other and when I get any news from an observation point, I merely send it back to our CP and it's then acted upon. But we are under artillery fire. Every once in a while I guess they lob a shell in our direction, but we won't worry about that right now, will we, Darling?
   I am living in a barn. It's more difficult to sleep because of artillery fire all night long. You'll probably think you're married to a bull before long since I'm constantly living in a barn.
   A shell just landed pretty close, Darling, and sort of shook us up a bit but it wasn't close enough to do any damage to us except scare the dickens out of us and make us hug the ground.

   "A bit? Are you kidding? It scared the crap out of us!"

   I'm glad you found out in the paper where I am because, you know, I don't want to keep any secrets from you and I can't tell you where I am but I can tell you it's hell. Every bit of it. I just hope it ends as soon as people think it will, but after you get into it and see how it's fought, it's a long way from being over.
   I'll have to close for now, my Darling, because it's going to rain and I have to set up my machine gun and dig a prone shelter, and

I want to get that done. So until later I'll sign off with loads and loads of love and kisses, darling.
    Your loving hubby,
    Sandy

Suddenly, for the first time in Sandy's life, someone was firing at him. Artillery shells whizzed all around, some landing as close as 50 yards away. Some of Sandy's buddies were hit. There was no place to go. The ground was flat as a pancake. Sandy wished he were back home working in his dad's grocery store. Beth was petrified and hung on inside Sandy's jacket pocket for dear life…literally.

Beth saw a guy Sandy had been talking to earlier lying in the snow, lifeless and bloody. Sandy started to run across the field in the twelve inches or so of snow to retrieve the body. As shots were fired, Sandy made a dive for a mound of dirt near the soldier. He lay there for about five minutes, then arose when there was a lull in the firing, then hoisted the body onto his shoulders and ran for his M8 car. Beth hung on, frightened beyond words, inside Sandy's pocket. Sandy jumped into the car, trying to figure out what to do next. There weren't many guys left. Sandy didn't know how many had been killed, maybe 30, maybe more. It was devastating and frightening. Sandy took the body to the medics' tent, then he and Beth remained in the car until the shooting finally stopped.

Later that night, in the somewhat safety of the woods, trucks brought more blankets. Sandy and Beth were freezing in a foxhole with Ketchum and Jackson. They awoke around 5:00 AM and were sent out in front of the lines as the others prepared for another attack. For some unknown reason, the Germans didn't attack. Surprisingly, a truck with roast beef sandwiches and water arrived. The soldiers were happy because they were starving and their canteens were frozen.

Suddenly the shelling began again and lasted for about twenty minutes. Sandy and Ketch moved in front of the lines to determine where the German army was situated. Their armored car had three guns in the turret with lots of fire power, and Sandy was in the turret with Lt. Stevens as Ketchum drove.

As they approached the area near the German army, a shell hit their car and flipped it over. Though Sandy, Ketchum, Dickie, and AJ got out safely, Beth could barely breathe from the fright. Out of the car, Sandy realized that Lt. Stevens wasn't with them. He was stuck under one of the guns that had come detached from the turret in the crash. The Germans were firing on them, and bullets were whizzing by! But Sandy turned around and climbed back into the car, found Lt. Stevens, and pulled him out. Lt. Stevens was severely injured, so Sandy carried him into a nearby foxhole for safety. As they jumped into the hole, the Germans fired and Lt. Stevens was hit. When the shelling ceased, Sandy picked him up and carried him the rest of the way to the medic tent. Lt. Stevens was killed, but Sandy would later receive the Bronze Star medal for heroism for trying to save him.

Beth was learning more about these young U.S. soldiers, most of whom were drafted. Very few had volunteered. These citizen soldiers were here to do the job they were told to do. They leave the relative safety of their foxholes, marching forward with machine guns, small arms, mortar, and artillery fire everywhere. Fear keeps them moving forward if they're not killed or wounded. There is no hope of transferring to safer circumstances. Combat is the only reality with no escape except by death, wounding, capture, mental breakdown, desertion or if one dared imagine, the end of the war. Sooner or later they will become a casualty—not *if* but *when*—yet they continue. They fight well as they move grimly forward to attack the enemy.

The Recons moved into a little town very close to Strasbourg, a beautiful old cathedral city—now mostly rubble—in the Alsace area, not far from the Rhine River, called Illkirk Grafanstaden They spent the next week there in preparation to move forward.

The men were billeted in a big two-story house, all assigned to one room where they had to sleep on the floor with nothing but a piece of canvas for a mattress.

"Sandy-boy," said AJ in his thick southern drawl. "You speak some German. How do you even pronounce the name of this place?"

Beth huffed a disgusted whisper into Sandy's ear. "Would you please tell that ignoramus that this is France, not Germany?"

"Uh, AJ, we're not in Germany yet. We're still in France. The name of this place is French. I think it's pronounced Illy-kirsh-gra-fan-staden. Beautiful name, beautiful place," said Sandy almost dreamily.

As Beth and Sandy and the men walked around, they saw that this place, this Illkirk Grafanstaden, was mostly destroyed with only a few buildings standing and none of the citizens in sight, if there were still any. They could hear shelling off in the distance. The house in which they were bunked, they agreed, had probably been a school, with what was left of pencils and papers and small tables and chairs.

That night, as Beth lay snuggled in Sandy's makeshift rolled up backpack that he used for a pillow, she began thinking about this place, this mostly bombed-out school. *Where are the children?* she wondered. *What happened to the kids who live, or lived, here? Where did they go?* She realized for the first time that she'd not thought about the children at all. She knew what had happened to Jewish children: they were sent to the concentration camps, tortured and killed. But what about the German and French children who lived in the bombed-out towns? Whenever her teachers and even her great-grandfather talked about the war back home, no one mentioned children, although once Pop talked about a little girl who liked him. She would explore these thoughts more, just as soon as she had a handle on what was happening here.

Bombed out town in France

The Recons moved into Strasbourg, France, and were taken to a synagogue to sleep. The synagogue was nearly destroyed because German soldiers had gone inside with machine guns and sprayed the walls. Regardless of the condition of the synagogue, it kept Sandy, Beth and the others out of the freezing weather for a while. They were able to get some much-needed sleep.

In her sleep, Beth dreamed that she saw soldiers getting wounded, getting killed. She watched the young soldiers, only a couple of years older than herself, struggle to stay alive, to do anything not to think about death. She dreamt about their need for diversion from the challenges of fighting, the fun in Paris and their talk about the sex they had there. She awoke, thought about her dream, and knew she was actually okay hearing the bravado and knowing that women in Paris were at least surviving with the income from the soldiers. And, as Beth learned, besides being incredibly homesick and deeply frightened every single day, the men could forget about the war for a few moments as sex is one of the activities that tends to put people in the present, in the now. Whatever helped these guys survive was okay with her.

Every day Sandy and the Recon men went into the Colmar region to determine the position of the German army. The Americans dug in defense positions as they kept the Germans from again advancing on Strasbourg from the south. The positions permitted Allied Forces to defend this important city though much of it had already been destroyed.

The Recons were given new M8 armored cars. Sandy was the radioman and gunner for his car which had a 3mm gun and two different radios to report back to the troops. The men in the car carried M1 carbines for action and self-defense outside of the car. Three M1A1 anti-tank mines were loaded onto each side of the car which had both top and front hatches. An open turret was located between them. A 37mm gun was elevated and rotated manually in the turret. The car was made from all-welded construction though the floor had rather thin armor. Sandy's team put sandbags on the floor to help protect them from land mines. On the front hull between the headlights were racks for six mines. The driver sat on the left and radio operator sat on the right. The driver used a standard steering wheel. Much of the crew's equipment had to be stored externally as there wasn't enough room inside the car. The car's fans were in the rear of the car and blew towards the rear, allowing for silent operation so the car could quietly approach the enemy.

M8 armored car

February 23, 1945
My Dearest Darling Lassie:

"Who's Lassie? What happened to Lois?
"Lassie is Lois's nickname. Quit bothering me."

Every night when I get in, which is usually between 12 and 2, I've been getting mail, and that does so much for morale. You'd be surprised. When I'm reading a letter from you, I can't even hear the shells explode or fly overhead, because it puts me far away from here, with you, Darling.
You know, Darling, I wasn't missed too far by a shell the other day.

"The damned thing practically landed on us!"

Shrapnel flew all over the place, but it didn't hurt anything.

"Yeah, except our nerves!"

I caught a piece of it. I was really scared there for a few minutes but I guess it's all in the game.

Last night as we were on duty, our bombers came over, a steady stream of them all over the skies for about a half an hour. Boy, was that a pretty sight. It's the largest flight I have ever seen, and it just sort of does things to you. It gives you a tingling sensation inside, just like you were in love with them or something.

You know, Darling, when I was in the States and hadn't seen you for a little while, I really missed you tremendously, but it wasn't half as much as I miss you over here although it's only about three months since I saw you. I miss you more than anyone can imagine. Every night as I lay here and gaze up at the sky, I can just picture us in our little home, and boy, it just makes me want to walk out on them and go home, but I know that would never do, so I guess I'll just have to keep sweating it out. I hope it's not for too long though.
So until later, my love, I'll close remaining,
Your loving hubby,
Sandy

Beth thought *I don't have the heart to tell him it'll be another year before he gets to go home.*

Beth was always surprised when Sandy shared his feelings. Most of the time he was stoic, unable or at least reluctant to express what was going on inside of himself. Yet when he shared his feelings, Beth noted, they were profound and tender. She wondered how he had become so reserved as the adult Sandy, her great-grandfather, who she knew so well. His letters to Lois were incredibly mushy, almost *yucky* in their sappiness, yet there was such a sweetness about them, about him. She began to develop an understanding of Sandy, an understanding that struck her hard in her head and in her heart.

Beth perceived herself to be a nerd, a geek, and totally out of place in her social environment. She wasn't interested in boys or makeup or dresses or school or anything, really, other than Hetalia, Manga, My Little Pony, and, of course, computers. She had few friends at school, though she had her girlfriend Nikki who she loved very much. Mostly she was involved with the on-line Hetalia community, isolating herself from much of the real world. Beth knew who she was and had a strong sense of self, but she felt alone and often abandoned by her mother. Beth and her mother were very much alike, though Beth didn't know this yet. Her mother and grandmother were alike as well, but Beth's mother would never admit it. All three women shared an unspoken sense of difference among peers, isolation from friends, and abandoned—but in different ways—from their mothers. Beth was drawn to her great-grandfather, loved the old man deeply, and needed to be on this journey with him. She just didn't realize that both she and her great-grandfather experienced a need to belong, a need be loved, a need to be respected among peers.

———————

Sandy's heavy recon activity continued. Among the men in his unit, there were some casualties and losses, but the enemy was repaid in kind. The German war machine was ground down by years of defeat and retreat. Tanks were short of fuel, artillery short of shells, and many of their soldiers had gone unpaid for months. Morale was shot by the streams of defeated refugees and walking cadavers, clogging the roads, leaving their destroyed hometowns. Yet they fought on. They fought with the courage of men with nothing left to lose.

———————

February 26, 1945
My Dearest Darling Wife:
I missed writing again yesterday but it couldn't be helped because there were so many other things that had to be done.

"Yeah, like killing people!"

I'm sure you understand. You're such a sweet little wife.

"Why do you say such stupid things sometimes? Sweet little wife? I'd dump your butt for sure with THAT one!"

Don't mind me too much if I say something that doesn't make any sense because I'm on duty now and am trying to listen for calls on the radio while writing to you.

86

Well, we're almost through with this first mission up here on the O.P. (observation post) *I guess we're through Wednesday and then another platoon takes over and we start on our second mission. I don't know exactly what it is, but maybe later I can tell you more about it. Our O.P. here is from an old castle. They claim it's about 900 years old. It looks it, even if it isn't actually that old. It has a moat around it just like you see in pictures of those old feudal castles and dungeons, and it sits right at the top of a hill, and you can see it for miles away. At a distance it looks like a small castle. It's really a nice sight.*

Last night when we got back to the O.P., instead of having to sleep in a barn, I had a bed to sleep in, in a room, and there are also chairs, a stove and a table there. It's the first time since I left the states that I slept in a bed and it felt so good that it hurt, no kidding, it was so soft and warm. You see, the people over here, all have these real thick feather beds and boy, are they comfortable. I guess I'll have to leave it soon, when we start our next mission.

I guess I'll have to close for now, Darling, because for one thing I can't think of anything else to write and for another thing, it's time for me to write a report, so until later, I'll close reminding you that I'll always love you very dearly, Darling.

With that thought in mind, I'll close again with loads of love and tons of kisses.
　　　　Your loving hubby,
　　　　Sandy

―――――――――

The fighting became intense. Sandy's second armored car was hit, and he and the others crawled out from under it, becoming easy targets. German troops opened fire with small arms and screaming mimis which were rocket artillery intended to deliver poison gas and smoke. The Rainbow soldiers fired heavy rounds back at them. Wounded German soldiers began coming out of the woods, hands up, calling "comrades." Beth looked back across the field and saw many men injured or dead. She was heartsick.

Night fell quickly. It was very dark and the temperature was way below zero...too cold to snow. The bright moonlight lit up the field. Men were moaning and crying as the medics arrived. Wounded men were lying on either side of Sandy and Beth and Ketchum, and they did what they could to help. Luckily, Dickie and AJ made it through without injuries and joined in to help Sandy and Ketch. When an armored car arrived, Dickie tried to get heat for the others by running the motor.

After the attack

February 28, 1945
My Dearest Darling Wife:
Last night the jerries laid down another barrage of fire on us, and I'm telling you, when that fire started I'm just like a ground hog or something. I stay close to the ground. In fact I stayed under the armored car all the time that I didn't have to be on the radio. All the wires had been blasted out of the castle except for the one I had, and I had to get a message through to headquarters, and I hated sitting in that car when those shells were landing so close. But I got it through and I guess everything turned out okay. No one got hurt or anything which is all that matters.

"You did a good job keeping us alive, Pop. I, for one, thank you."

Today is a beautiful day, Darling, almost like a spring day. It's the kind of day that makes me wish that I was with you. I like spring better than any other season of the year. I sure hope that by next spring we are together again so we can do our spring house cleaning together.

The people in this house are swell people. They're an old couple and every morning they bring us up a pitcher of hot milk, but I never drink any of it because milk can cause two different diseases if it isn't pasteurized. But they're awfully disappointed if we don't take it. The old man chops wood for us. But just the same, you don't trust these people. They are Germans, and when the Nazis were here, they flew the swastika. Now they're flying the stars and stripes.

I have to close for now, darling, so until later, I'll close loving you with all my heart.

> *Your loving hubby,*
> *Sandy*

Sandy's unit was billeted in a farmhouse overnight. The day of fighting had been the worst Sandy had experienced. Beth remembered shells bursting and bodies flying in the air. By the time they found this little village, they were exhausted. The men asked the townspeople for food. The people were frightened of the Americans. Hitler had said that Americans would torture them, so they didn't give them food, but they told the men where they could steal chickens and watermelon.

Beth watched the men make friends with people in the village, eating with them when they finally did offer what little food they had. They laughed and joked with them as they ate. That night, the soldiers ambushed that very same village because the German army had arrived. As the fight began, the enemy retreated into the village. Three U.S. artillery strikes left the town flattened. Smoke and dust filled the air. Beth's heart was penetrated to the very depths of her soul seeing that destruction, having enjoyed the day with the people who lived there, the people now dead. Could she stay here long enough to get her questions answered?

Beth began to think more deeply about war. Meaning must be found in the act of killing, even in war. These young men were killing other young men, perhaps some just like themselves. Grief and mourning for their buddies who were killed overtook the men, and yet they did everything they could not to feel their emotions. Grief was deadened by alcohol, drugs, violence, and empty sex, as Beth observed. She wondered how anyone can expect a normal 18-year-old to kill someone then continue life in a healthy way? Drugs, alcohol, and suicide were among the ways the soldiers avoided their overwhelming feelings of grief and guilt.

When Beth tried to share some of her thoughts with Sandy, especially to find out how he was holding up, he merely said, "I'm okay. Pulling the trigger wasn't as hard as I thought it would be. Except for the first one."

The soldiers became convinced that the Germans were inferior life forms, not truly human; scapegoating at its finest. Their natural resistance to killing human beings was reduced by referring to them only as *krauts* or *jerries*. Denying the German soldiers' humanity by referring to them with disrespectful names made it easier somehow. Killing an enemy, therefore, was not about taking a life but rather stopping a threat that might save the lives of your buddies.

When they had a break the next evening, Beth again asked Sandy how he was doing. Sandy thoughtfully replied. "I'm okay, I guess. It's all so awful, so I try not to think about what I'm doing. I just do what I'm told. One thing's kind of funny. Since I'm the only Jew in the unit, the other soldiers bring German prisoners to me and say *Jude*. That's all it takes. The German soldiers look terrified, and they should! The guys felt that as long as our prisoners know I'm Jewish, they won't give us any trouble. And they don't! The prisoners are afraid of me." Sandy thought about what he had said and added, " I could just as soon kill them as not."

Sandy continued. "But I don't hate all Germans. Remember earlier, Beth, when we entered that farmhouse? I was prepared to kill everyone inside so we could hide. Remember? I asked the German family living there whether there were any German soldiers around. They said no but that the German army was coming this way. We were kind of rough with them at first, but they took us and hid us from the German soldiers and, maybe because I was the youngest, they treated me well. The walls in their bedroom were lined with drawers. So while the rest of the men hid in the barn, that family hid you and me and Ketch in that massive chest of drawers in the bedroom. The family told us when it was safe to come out. Remember? So maybe some Germans aren't all bad."

Beth knew that Sandy didn't want or need a response. He was trying to make sense of something that was totally senseless. He needed to say something nice about the enemy.

After the fighting ceased in Hatten, Beth walked down the main street to see the remains of this little town. At the end of the street was a silk factory, the largest source of employment in town. A half-ton bomb had dropped in front of it, killing or injuring nearly everyone inside. Bodies were blown 200 yards along the street. Some ended up in the city park about 300 feet away. One dead girl was found outside a nearby house. The power of the blast had blown her through an open window.

There was a girl about Beth's age standing in front of a bombed-out house, cuts and bruises all over her face. Beth, extended to her full size, asked the girl if she needed help. She looked at Beth, at the strange American girl who spoke German.

"A bomb came through the roof of my house. My dressing table and clothes are in shreds. Windows are blown out, and all the legs are missing from my bed. The mattress is hanging partly out of my window. My mother was killed. Please, no more bombs, no more fighting, no more soldiers, no more falling into ditches full of death."

Beth listened as the young woman talked, almost to no one in particular. "The bombing was so immense that houses shook, pictures fell from the wall, and telephones rang with no one there. I heard the rumblings of the planes, felt the building shake, and knew that our time had come. And throughout it all, because it's gone on for so damned long, we stand in ration lines, women and girls, and ask each other if the Americans would please get here before the Soviets do. The Soviet troops steal and rape. The Americans are here now. I hope they treat us better than the Soviets."

Beth could feel the rumble as planes filled the air. Sandy and the men saw their first dogfight between an American P47 plane and a German fighter, right over their heads! None of the young soldiers had ever seen a fight between airplanes before. They were both frightened and awed.

Sandy stood in the middle of the street, mouth open, watching the planes until Ketchum screamed for him to jump to safety, just before a German plane strafed the streets with bullets. With Beth securely back in his pocket, Sandy tumbled under his armored car.

"Holy shit! Did you see that???" he hollered excitedly to Ketchum and anyone else within the sound of his voice.

"Yeah, and we nearly saw you get taken out! Damn, Sandy, don't stand there and watch what's happening or you'll never see the light of tomorrow!"

Beth had to re-catch her breath. *Holy shit is right*, she thought. *We almost bought THAT one. I can't let this dude get us killed or there won't BE an us!* She clutched her chest, unable to speak, and worked on regaining her composure.

All daylight movement was stopped. Now the soldiers traveled in the darkness of the freezing nights. Because Sandy, Ketch, AJ, and Dickie were Reconnaissance, they drove their M8 car in front of the lines, ahead of the soldiers, mapping the roads and reporting enemy movement back to the commanding officers. Snow and ice were everywhere.

The soldiers put the heavy combat field packs on their backs as they prepared to move forward. The packs contained necessities like underwear, a mess kit (short for abbreviated plates, forks, cups, and the smallest can-opener Beth ever saw), and toilet articles, along with a poncho and bedroll strapped to the outside. In addition to the bulky packs, the men wore big overcoats that came down to their knees, a field jacket, a wool shirt, and pants. They also had on long underwear and combat boots with heavy socks…everything they needed to survive outdoors in the bitter cold. But at the last minute, the soldiers were instructed to leave their packs behind. The packs were too heavy and would slow down their movement too much.

Heavy fog had formed during the night and the ground was thick with deep snow. As they headed to the battlefront, the infantry was in the lead, but Sandy's recon unit was ahead of the infantry.

More snow was accumulating on the ground, if that were even possible, and the temperature was at zero degrees. The tanks had trouble moving very far because of the thick ice and the heavy guns and equipment. The going was extremely slow.

As Reconnaissance soldiers in the infantry, Sandy, Ketchum, AJ, and Dickie rode in the M8 armored car ahead of the troops, searching for the enemy, for unclogged routes, and for safe places to stop. Sandy operated the car radio. He received a message that was to be given to the commanding officer. He read it out loud to the men and, of course, Beth heard—and commented:

1. There should be more Bazookas in the Rifle companies (*Great*, thought Beth. *Just how are they supposed to carry them?*) and ammunition for them must be obtained (*Yeah? Like, from where? Guns R Us France??*). All personnel must know how to fire this weapon. *(Except they forgot to teach this class.)* They must be employed to knock out enemy armor and be able to move to other concealed positions before enemy foot troops can move in to stop these tactics. (*Swell, as IF anyone could move in this weather mess!*) AT rifle grenades must supplement the Bazooka and can be employed only against very vulnerable parts of tanks. Bazookas must be kept at the Command Posts also as protection. (*What are the soldiers supposed to do? Check them out???*)

2. Tank support must maintain close liaison with the infantry battalion it is supporting. They cannot pull out or change positions without knowledge of the Battalion Commander of Infantry. (*They need to ask permission???*)

3. At least one day's emergency food and water rations must be kept on all defensive positions.

4. An individual weapon with an accurate range of 300 yards or more is desired. (*Getting out of Europe is even more desired by these guys!*) A weapon similar to the Fromusket or other larger caliber recoilless weapon is recommended.

5. Alternate Battalion Aid Stations are recommended, and to be located away from all Command Posts. Jerry knows our habits of Aid Stations close to Command Posts. (*Who told Jerry???*)

6. Small towns on or near the lines should be cleared of civilians. (*Cleared of civilians? What the hell happened to the children? Were they among the civilians who were 'cleared?' And what, exactly, did 'cleared' mean?*) They are very good snipers, and would no doubt give information to the enemy about our installations.

Beth took the time to really look at the next bombed-out town. There were eerie scenes of people huddling around outdoor cooking fires, families occupying homes with missing walls and exposed rooms. Hungry people emerged from underground hovels to wonder around heaps of bricks that entombed their neighbors. Staircases led to empty air. Lacking money, cigarettes were used as currency. Water was undrinkable, and the few remaining residents of the city were angry and dangerous. The place smelled of dust, infection, and death. Is this what was meant by *cleared of civilians*?

———————————

As the troops moved forward, they stopped in the evenings for some sleep even though they could hear bombs and gunfire in the distance.

"Pop, what were you like as a kid?" Beth had become curious about her great-grandfather's life and wanted to think about something other than this horrifying war.

Sandy pondered the question for a minute. Then he said, "I'm still a kid, but I guess in age only now. I feel kind of old, actually."

"Do you have many friends back home? What do you do for fun?"

Sandy thought for a long while and sounded almost sad when he spoke. "I don't really have friends back home. Oh, I know lots of people, probably everyone in town, but my job was always to look out for my sisters and kid brother. No one is more important than family."

"How did, er, does that feel to you? Did you *want* to be responsible for them or did you want to go play with the other boys?"

"I had no choice. I *had* to be responsible for them. My father works all the time to take care of the family and my mother speaks very little English. As the oldest son, it's my job. Nobody told me to do it. I just knew I was supposed to. I didn't really have the time to go play with other kids, anyway, because I also worked in my dad's store. And now I'm married."

"But, Pop, how do you *feel* about it all?"

"I guess I wouldn't say this to anyone else but since you're not real, I'll tell you. I feel angry a lot. I feel alone a lot, even in a big family. I feel different from any of my friends. I want to be loved and I want to be respected. I married Lois because I deeply love her and I know I'll go home to her, if she doesn't leave me for someone who's already back from the war, but I don't think anyone really respects me for anything. I guess that's one of the reasons I'm here…to get respect from my father."

"Do you honestly think Lois will run off with someone else? C'mon, Pop, get real!"

"I don't know. Some of these guys here, they're messing with the local girls. Some even said they're going to divorce their wives and come back for the girl here, and some of the single ones want to take the girl back to the States, for cryin' out loud!"

"Dude! Listen to yourself! None of that has anything to do with your wife leaving YOU for someone else. Are you really that insecure?"

Then Beth got quiet, even thoughtful for a few moments. "Sorry, Pop," she said softly, then spoke slowly. "Pop, I feel the exact same way." Her voice was almost tearful. "I feel so alone even when I'm with my family and my few friends. I feel so different from them. I know some of them, especially my Grandma, your oldest daughter, loves me fiercely, and so does my girlfriend Nikki, but otherwise, I just feel like a jerk most of the time. So awkward. My mom and step-dad think I'm a big loser and my dad, who does love me, is as weird as me except he has lots of friends just like himself. My little sister is the only one who knows me well and loves me for who I am, sometimes even when I don't love myself. And respect? Shit—oh, sorry—no one respects me for anything, not even for my brains. I don't know my place in the world so I do cosplay, that costume play I told you about, with other nerds like myself. It keeps my brain functioning far beyond kids in my school. I know that, but it also makes me different from them. Isolated, really."

Beth was silent again then said "Damn, Pop, we're three generations apart in age yet so much alike. I don't know if that's good or bad, but it's the truth…" Her voice trailed off and they both sat quietly together.

———————————

Sandy thought about the question Beth had asked him several times: *why are you here? Why are you fighting?* He also thought about Beth herself, still disbelieving that she was anything more than his imagination. But he wanted—no, needed—to answer her question. He thought of his father and the letter he had received five years earlier from that Care organization that said to stop sending money to the family in Poland because there was no one left. *Yes, I'm here because I want to get even,* Sandy thought. *It's that simple.*

————————————

Beth wasn't the only avatar floating around Europe during those last few months of the war. While she was brilliant enough to create her avatar, others were equally as intelligent…and courageous. The information they obtained by hacking into DARPA to get the U.S. government's protocol for creating avatars was a piece of cake for the *Hetalia* teens. Beth's timing and abilities were coordinated with an entire underground of young people like herself who were curious, of course, but more importantly, demanded to know why the Holocaust happened. They simply could not understand how an entire generation of people could be wiped out, how the Nazis could be so cruel, and why young soldiers from their respective countries would agree, regardless of being drafted with little choice, to go into hand-to-hand combat thousands of miles from their homes. These were questions that must be answered, questions that guided the avatars' quest.

Two Hetalia cosplay avatars were from England, two from France, and one each from Germany, Italy, Switzerland, Canada and Austria. Only Beth was from the U.S., a total of ten avatars, all with the same abilities, all with the same desires to know, and with a giant dose of courage. All had a soldier with whom they were partnered, but Beth was the only avatar who was with an actual family member.

The reason the avatars went back to WWII Europe was to try to understand and to see the truth for themselves, whatever that truth might be. They had specific questions whose answers they sought, but those questions raised even more issues for them. They wanted to learn how and why the Nazis killed so many people and why American soldiers were there despite the U.S. government's desire to remain isolated from Europe. As the avatars experienced the battles, heard the stories, and saw first-hand the horror of war, Beth began to wonder why the U.S. didn't get involved sooner. Did President Roosevelt not know what was happening? How could that be? She forgot that there was not the instant communication of the internet or computers with which she lived her daily life. But, still, she found it puzzling that the U.S. didn't act sooner. The avatars decided to explore libraries and universities, whatever remained standing, to learn more of the historical information that led up to the Holocaust and the U.S. involvement, or lack thereof, during that time.

They decided to split the task and focus on their own countries. They also wanted to find out what happened to the children who remained in the towns that had been destroyed in battle. Did they flee? To where? Or were they hiding in the remaining nooks and crannies for safety? Or were they dead?

Beth was eager to learn…

9.

The Story of the Holocaust

Beth left Sandy and went alone up the road to Schweinfurt, Germany on the Main River. Schweinfurt was a town with a 1200-year history but was now an industrial center with several ball-bearings plants for the German military. Or at least it was before it was destroyed. People lived in relative prosperity here before WWII, but the town had repeatedly been bombed, day and night, for the last two years to stop Germany from building more planes. Before the Allied air forces bombed the crap out of it, Schweinfurt's economy was robust. Now most of Schweinfurt was in ruins. Thousands of its citizens were killed or severely maimed. And in the worst moments of the war, Russian, German, and even Allied soldiers were terribly abusive to the women and girls of Schweinfurt.

As Beth entered Schweinfurt, she transformed into her full-size five-foot-eight teenage self, wearing her Beth America cosplay outfit. She put out a call on her wrist phone to the other Hetalia cosplay avatars who might be nearby. She didn't want to search for and find the children of the town by herself. She didn't know what she'd learn, but her gut wasn't happy. She couldn't do it alone. Ludvig Germany and Kate Canada answered her call and arrived immediately. They met Beth at the entrance to the pile of rubble of what had been the #3 ball-bearing plant.

"Thanks so much for coming," greeted Beth. "I'm Beth America. I'm here to learn more about this war because of those despicable Holocaust deniers back home in the U.S."

"I'm Ludvig," said the German avatar. "My great-grandfather is dead now but he fought with the German army, and I need to know more. No one in my family has ever talked about it. I'm almost scared to learn anything about this, but I know it's important for me." Beth thought Ludvig looked pretty cool in his turquoise military suit. It had a white-on-black lining on the collar, shoulder, and cuffs, and he wore a leather waist belt and chest strap. His spikey black hair completed the look. Beth knew a bit about Ludvig, like he's not great about interacting with people, but he speaks German and would be helpful with translation. Though Beth as an avatar could speak and understand most languages, she was grateful that Ludvig had joined her. Besides, she thought, he's cute. Beth had a girlfriend back home, but she appreciated attractive guys, too.

"I'm Kate. So happy to meet both of you. Thanks for putting out the call, Beth." Kate Canada was in her gray wool jumpsuit with a white collared shirt, a red necktie, and a red and white overcoat with a Canadian maple leaf on each pocket. "You two have great-grandparents fighting here. I don't, but I want to help, and like you, I want to know more."

"Have you guys been in any of the war zones?" asked Beth. "I've seen some real shit since I got here in January."

"Seriously," responded Kate. "There's some terrible, horrible, disgusting stuff going on here. I hate seeing it, but I can't seem to leave. It's got me so sucked in."

"If it's that bad for you two, just think how bad it is for me," said Ludvig in a quiet voice. "These are my people. Some of them are good people doing bad things, some are bad people doing horrendous things, and some are good people trying to do good things but are getting brutalized for it. I'm so hurt, so embarrassed, and just can't imagine…" His words trailed off, exposing the pain in his heart.

All three avatars came from 2017. All had learned about the World War II that occurred 70-some years earlier, but none of them could fathom the atrocities they had already witnessed and those about which they would learn.

Beth spoke. "Look, we know how it turns out, how many millions of people are killed, and that some assholes back home are denying that it even happened. I wish we had some way of making it all better but, really, all we can do is observe stuff here and share it with people back home in 2017. That's why I want to talk with some of the kids. It's nearly impossible to find stories about their lives. I want to know, and to make sure others know. I had relatives killed in the concentration camps. I can't let the deniers get away with their lies."

Kate looked at Ludvig. All three avatars, now in their full-size selves, were in agreement. "We're with you, Beth. This is your operation. Take the lead and let's do it," said Kate. Ludvig nodded his approval.

"Okay. Ludvig, we need to find young people like ourselves. Male, female, I don't care. Let's just see if we can find anyone alive and willing to talk. I brought a bunch of food for them. Those K-rations the army guys get are disgusting but edible, and the people here are starving."

"How'd you get those, Beth? Good thinking!"

" My Pop helped me, uh, requisition, several dozen packages over the past two months."

"What's a pop?" asked Kate.

"Oh, that's my great-grandfather. His name is Sandy but we call him Pop." She thought for a moment. "It's weird. I know him in real life back home as an old man who tells stories about the war, but right now I get to hang out with him as some dude who's only a couple of years older than me. I know times are different, but, damn, the guy is such a dork! Sweet, but a dork." Kate and Ludvig laughed, both envious that Beth was in Europe with someone she loved. And simply by her presence, they knew Sandy survived.

Ludvig said, "We should be able to find kids, Beth, though I doubt any will be boys. Nearly all the boys older than eight were taken by the Hitler Youth, made into child-soldiers, and probably dead by now. But let's see what we can do. Let's go."

As the avatars walked through town in search of teens with whom to talk, they noticed the condition of what was once an important, vibrant town. They saw rotting corpses of elderly people and very young children on the sides of the road, probably dead from starvation. The stench was sickening. People here were victims of years of aerial bombings and in-town fighting. They saw a woman with empty sleeves where her arms should have been. A body hung from the remains of a staircase that used to be inside a now-crumbled house.

The ice of the frozen winter was melting, and the constant rain made the narrow streets muddy. Shutters from houses still standing hung in strange formations exposing ragged curtains. Charred books poked out of the rubble in the streets that once were neighborhoods.

The avatars passed what must have been the town hall. They stopped at the one remaining wall that held two charred posters. One poster was a bulletin that listed the names of German soldiers from Schweinfurt who were killed in action. The other was a caricature of a Jewish man with a large round-brimmed hat, pockmarked cheeks, big lips, and a crooked beak nose. There was a yellow Star of David on his coat that said *Jude.* A large powerful-looking hand was pointing a finger down at the cowering man. The poster read *He is guilty for the war.* Another poster's image was burned, but the words were still readable:

The Jew is the parasite among humans. Beth was disgusted. *Such hateful bigots*, she thought.

Not far from the center of town the avatars passed what they recognized what must have been a synagogue though not much was left of it. They continued to walk as Ludvig explained the history that was responsible for the stories they were soon going to hear. He began:

"World War II was the most destructive war in human history. Over 55 million killed, more money spent, more property damaged, and more changes took place than ever before. Germany attacked Poland on September 1, 1939, then Denmark, Norway, Belgium, Luxembourg, The Netherlands, and France within the next three months. Japan attacked Pearl Harbor on December 7, 1941, where 2,400 people—mostly Americans—were killed, and nearly 20 American ships and more than 300 airplanes damaged or destroyed. Four days later both Japan and Germany declared war on the United States.

When World War I was over in 1919, the Treaty of Versailles banned all German military activity. Germany was bankrupt, had high unemployment, and German people were poor and desperate. They blamed the new German government for accepting the detested treaty, and needed someone to give them hope. When the government began to lose power, brash Adolph Hitler and his National Socialist (Nazi) party grew strong and offered the needed hope for a prosperous future.

Hitler was born in 1889 in Vienna. Though he had not completed school, he was a powerful motivational speaker. During his time in prison for treason, he wrote *Mein Kampf* in which he blamed the Jews for everything wrong in the world, described his hatred of the Jews, and documented his desire to eliminate them. Once out of prison, using his leadership in the disorganized German Worker's Party, Hitler created a boycott of Jewish businesses followed by sporadic violence. Soon, decrees stripped Jews of their rights and property, and, by 1935, Jews lost their German citizenship. Hitler promised that he would end the humiliating conditions that the defeat in WWI caused Germany, and created a common enemy of the Jews.

Adolf Hitler was sworn in as Chancellor of Germany on January 30, 1933. On February 27th, there was an arson fire at the German Parliament, or Reichstag, Building, which Hitler used as evidence that the Communists, who wanted expansion into Germany, were beginning to plot against the German Government. The next day Hitler convinced President Paul von Hindenburg to pass an emergency decree that suspended civil liberties and allowed the government to institute mass arrests of Communists and anyone else who they felt was a threat to Germany.

Hitler created a step-by-step process to destroy German Jewish communities. On April 1, 1933, there was a one-day boycott of Jewish businesses. On May 10, 1933, a massive book burning of mostly Jewish authors took place across Germany. Books by Einstein, Freud, and many other Jewish authors were burned as well as works by Hemingway and Helen Keller. Jews were banned from journalism, broadcasting, the theater, and even farming, and laws were created to increase the severity and scope of discrimination and persecution.

The Nuremberg Laws, created on September 15, 1935, segregated Jews from the German people, removing Jews from German citizenship. The Laws defined Jews by blood: If one had three Jewish grandparents, one was a Jew regardless of the religion one currently practiced.

The elimination of Jewish communities began with *Kristallnacht*, the night of broken glass, on November 9, 1938. Jewish stores and businesses were destroyed all over Germany. Windows were smashed and glass crunched under people's feet as they walked on the sidewalks. The German people laughed at what was a carnival atmosphere while police just looked on. German people with Jewish friends could do nothing to help.

Over the next two days, more than 1400 synagogues, including the one in Schweinfurt, were destroyed. Torah scrolls were stomped on and burned along with songbooks and the small tefillin boxes that held Torah verses. Over 30,000 Jewish boys and men were arrested by the SS and sent to concentration camps. By the time it was over, more than 7,500 businesses throughout Germany were destroyed along with Jewish cemeteries, hospitals, and schools. Homes were ransacked, and many were destroyed."

Ludvig stopped to catch his breath. Beth and Kate were stunned by the story, unable to comprehend the severity and the enormity of what they were hearing. He continued:

"Germany became a police state, and people's lives were now controlled by the Nazis and the secret police called the Gestapo. Trade unions were disbanded and their members were arrested and sent to work camps. German teachers and university professors who were anti-Nazi were replaced with Nazi supporters. Children were subjected to Nazi ideas and were taught to report their parents to the Gestapo if they said anything negative against Hitler or the Nazis. Children were told that Jews were inferior, that they were a criminal race and a grave danger to the German people.

While Jews were the primary target of the Nazis, they weren't the only ones. Communists, liberals, socialists, trade unionists, Jehovah's Witnesses, homosexuals, and Sinti people (called Gypsies) were also persecuted and sent to concentration camps. Germans who were mentally or physically challenged or emotionally disturbed—and therefore not suitable for breeding for the master race—were also sent to concentration camps, but most were killed before they ever arrived. Polish people were either killed or sent to the camps as were Soviet prisoners of war.

No one had enough power or courage to stop Hitler. Democracy in Germany was quickly destroyed with no challenge from anyone. Critics were murdered. With increasing hostility throughout Germany, Jews began to leave in large numbers but in 1941, all emigration was stopped.

Nazis arrested and murdered their fellow German citizens gruesomely and publically if they were suspected of harboring Jews or Allied soldiers. In addition, relatives and friends of the suspects were sent to concentration camps where many died.

By 1942, Jews were being sent by the thousands to the death camps and executed. The murder of all Jews was carried out with maximum efficiency and minimum use of resources. The "Final Solution" was the concentrated Nazi plan to exterminate all Jewish people in Europe through horrible acts of terror. Six million Jews, about two-thirds of European Jewry, were killed. In all of WWII, over 55 million people died. And if those who died from disease and famine are included, over 80 million people perished between 1933 and 1945...at the hands of my family."

Ludvig finished his historical summary, put his head in his hands, and cried. Beth and Kate were already crying. The three teenagers from 2017 simply could not fathom how the Holocaust could have taken place, how people could have carried it out, then live with such cruelty. They pondered if it could happen again.

"It has," Beth reminded them. She was thoughtful for a moment, but anger took her voice. Between clenched teeth, she rhetorically asked, "What about Pol Pot's Khmer Rouge in Cambodia in 1975 where probably three million people died? Or the Ethiopian Red Terror in 1977 where half a million people were killed? Or Rwanda in 1994 where a million people were slaughtered? Or Darfur, or Iraq, or Bosnia, or Bangladesh? And Syria! All of these were after WWII! So yes, damn it, we forgot, and it happened again and again! My question is this: Can it happen in our home countries in our generation? Can it happen in the U.S. or in Canada or even in Germany again?"

Beth was learning quite a bit about WWII and the existence of the Holocaust. She also knew that the soldiers she'd met while she was here, including Sandy himself, knew absolutely nothing about it. Not yet. They just knew that they were drafted, had a job to do, and hoped like hell to survive long enough to get home and start their lives.

Beth put her arms around her two new friends. They stood quietly in each others' arms until their tears subsided. The three avatars were feeling angry, sad, overwhelmed and helpless. They decided to leave Schweinfurt for now and meet up again in Mainz in early April.

10.

MARCH, 1945:

BIRTHDAY, HOLIDAY, HELL

The winter was exceptionally harsh, and temperatures were well below zero. At least two feet of snow covered the icy ground. Soldiers were paralyzed both by the cold and by fear. Given the chance to rest for several days, most stayed with their buddies in the combat zone. Food, beer, and mail helped alleviate some of the fear, at least momentarily. Beer was rationed at three bottles per week per man. The only thing more important than beer was mail. Mail was the assurance that the soldiers hadn't been forgotten, that there was a wife or a girlfriend or someone special somewhere in the world waiting for them to come home. "Dear John" letters, which informed a soldier that his girlfriend or wife was leaving him, affected the morale of an entire company. The biggest handicap for American troops was the never-ending homesickness.

      After each fight, teams of soldiers searched the battlefields for the dead. If the fight was still going on, the dead were quickly buried with a white stake placed into the ground near their head. A grave registration team would come back, dig up the body, and load it onto a truck. The body would be cleaned and fingerprinted. Pockets were emptied, dog tags removed, and personal effects were put into a paper bag. Before personal effects were sent home, soldiers would go through the pockets of the deceased to make sure there was nothing— such as contraceptives or pornography or address books or letters and photographs—that might betray an affair with a girl overseas only to cause grief with the solder's wife or girlfriend. The body was then put into a mattress cover and placed in a simple pine coffin. The dog tag would be sent home to the family.

      March was a deadly month.

———————————

      Beth and Sandy were awestruck. Beth whispered, "I've never seen a real castle before!" Sandy's duty took him into the medieval

Haut-Koenigsbourg castle near Colmar in the Alsace region of France. It was dark and damp and cob-webby, and creaking sounds were everywhere.

"I think it's haunted," whispered Beth. She was distressed that she was so frightened, given her family's obsession with HellView, the Halloween scare-house her father builds in her own yard every year!

"I remember I saw this castle in a movie once, a long time ago," Sandy recalled. "It was called *The Grand Illusion* or something like that. I can't believe I'm in this thing for real."

Beth noticed that Sandy and his men remained quiet while doing their work rather than engaging in their usual nervous banter. *I think this place is affecting all of us. So much history here,* she thought.

March 1, 1945
My Dearest Darling Wife:
    When I went on duty at the castle today, Darling, we had only been there for a couple of hours and the General sent an order for us to abandon the castle because it was too dangerous. We weren't too sorry about that, but I guess we'll have to go out and find a new operations post tomorrow.
    Well, if I keep up, Darling, I think I'll have a waistline as small as yours. You remember back in the States I had my 34 waist then down to a 32? Now even the 32 pants are too large for me. Oh well, I'll fatten up when I come home and eat your cooking, huh, Darling?
    I must close for now. I love you very much.
    Your loving hubby,
    Sandy

"Hey, Skinny, why didn't you tell her more about that creepy castle? And what happens if Lois is a lousy cook? No answers needed. Just sayin'..." Sandy just rolled his eyes at Beth.

For the first half of March 1945, the 42nd Division aggressively patrolled France and parts of Austria as they marched toward Germany, making deep penetrations behind enemy lines. During the first few days of March, sporadic gun and mortar blasts were heard. While Sandy conducted Reconnaissance patrolling, the rest of the troop engaged in training for the arduous march over rough terrain. The preparations played on the men's nerves.

In trying to get Sandy not to worry, because he always does, Beth asked about the salute Sandy uses to acknowledge officers. It was different from the salutes of men in other units.

"What's with your weird salute, Pop?" she asked.

Sandy pondered about the unique Rainbow salute. "I like our salute. It's different from the other divisions. We don't tilt our head back 45 degrees when saluting like the others do. We do the manly thing and look directly into the eyes of the person being saluted. I like that. It feels important." Dickie, who overheard the conversation, agreed. "Yeah, it's a good salute."

AJ changed the subject. "I've decided I'm gonna go AWOL if it gets too bad. I just wanna play my squeeze box, drink a little liquor, and mess with pretty women, in that order." Beth rolled her eyes. *He's got such ambition*, she thought sarcastically.

Ketch complained about dinner. "That steak supper tonight, I dunno, it seemed awfully tough. I complained to the cook." He laughed. "He apologized, took it back, and brought me a new one."

"Like hell he did!" grinned Dickie. "He probably slapped you silly with it." Everyone laughed.

Sandy suggested a round of cribbage, a game he had recently learned. The board was small, about eight inches long and three inches wide with pegs so small the men could barely maneuver them in their fingers. But they managed, and they played as often as possible to while away the time. Drinks and cribbage, a good way to forget for a moment that gunfire was not far off in the distance. Some of the men went to the main tent to watch George Gershwin's film *Rhapsody in Blue.*

Beth watched these young men and listened to their banter. Every one of them was scared to death, and none had yet been able to answer the question of why they were there. They didn't really want to go to war, but they didn't try to avoid service either. It was their job, these citizen soldiers. They'd do their job and then go home, they hoped. It was that simple, but still no answer as to why they were there.

Suddenly a long barrage of fire hailed on them and lasted into the morning. As the fire began, they pushed backward to a safer area. No one was injured.

"I hate backtracking like that," Sandy complained. "We need to keep moving forward." There was bravado in his voice, but also an urgency Beth hadn't heard before.

They found themselves in another little French village.

———————

Mar. 2, 1045
My Dearest Darling Wife:

Some little kid just brought me an apple. It tastes pretty good, too. The people act nice enough toward us, but as far as being friendly with them, we just don't do that.

One of the fellows that lives across the street from us has gotten so friendly with the woman there that she wants to marry him and come back to the states with him and just keep house for him. That's all she wants to do. The old lady where I live came up to bring us a pitcher of milk this morning and saw us washing some clothes and she insisted on doing it. So you see how these French people are here.

Well, my Darling, I guess I have to close for now as I do have to eat and then there'll probably be something for me to do after I eat.

Until tomorrow or maybe later today, Darling, I close loving you very dearly. Loads of hugs and kisses,
Your loving hubby,
Sandy

———————

Several days later, after no more firing was heard, movement began, and the front lines were reshuffled. Sandy and his Recon men were ready for combat patrolling. Their unit was bunkered in a house in the middle of the woods, near absolutely nothing at all. The little wooden house, no larger than an eight foot by ten foot room, was falling apart from neglect and from the freezing ice that was imbedded in every nook and cranny outside and in. The winter remained harsh, and the men couldn't get warm.

"Let's get a fire going in that thing," said Dickie, referring to the fireplace.

"Can't," answered Ketch. If we light that sucker, one of two things will happen. Either the jerries will see the light and blow us to smithereens, or this shack burns down and we're sitting ducks. I don't like either option."

March 5, 1945
My Dearest Darling Wife:

    I'm sorry I haven't written in the past few days but we moved again and so I didn't have any time for anything. I told you that we were going to start a new mission. Well, we have. I'm closer to the front lines now than I was before but we've got a pretty good setup here. Our job is to patrol the roads, and there are three of us operators working the radios. We have a radio room to ourselves and we all take shifts. It's okay but we never get a full night's sleep. We're living out in the wilderness now in a small house. You don't see anyone and no one sees us, which I don't mind at all, since I have to be over here.

    I got your birthday card, Darling, and it sure was clever. I love everything about you, but that's only natural because you're wonderful, as if I had to tell you.

    Today we were told that if any of us operators violate signal security while transmitting a message, we will be court martialed. They're really scaring us. They'll have it so that we'll be afraid to go near the radio pretty soon. Between them and the enemy, we'll be nervous wrecks before long.

    I go on shift for four hours at 12:00 tonight. I'll have to close until later. Until then, I'll close loving with all my heart as always and wishing you pleasant dreams.

    Your loving hubby,
    Sandy

"When's your birthday, Pop? Why did you get that card now?" asked Beth.

"March 13th. I'll be 20 years old. Sure wish I was home to celebrate it with Lois and my family," Sandy said sullenly. "How old did you say you are?"

"I'm 17, Pop. I'll be 18 in May. Not much younger than you. Just very different."

"I'll say…," Sandy half whispered.

———————

As the unit moved backward again to avoid enemy fire, they found themselves in Colmar, not far from the castle in which they had worked a few days earlier.

March 6, 1945
My Dearest Darling Wife:

Well, here I am back in the same village that I left the other day. We were called back today from that other mission. They've got something else for us. I can't tell you exactly what it is right at present, I don't believe, but you'd sure get a big kick out of it. I'll be able to tell you about it in due time. It ought to be interesting if it doesn't get us down in a hurry.

I'm living in another place in the village now since someone else has taken our other room. I guess it was a stable once or something like that, but we've got it fixed up okay to live in for awhile. Boy, I'm sure glad you can't see some of these places that I've lived in in the past couple of months, but they're a lot better than living in a fox-hole as the infantry does. We at least can rig up some kind of light and have some heat.

Don't forget to send me some film every once in a while, Darling because there are some pretty interesting things to take pictures of and send to you. For instance some of those places where I've lived over here and that old castle.

I have to get some sleep now, Darling. I expect a pretty tiring day tomorrow. Until later, Darling, I close loving you as always.

> *Your loving hubby,*
> *Sandy*

"Holy shit!" Beth and Sandy exclaimed together. The "other mission" to which Sandy referred in his letter to Lois involved donkeys! "Seriously???" Beth asked. "We have to, uh, ride these things? To where?" Sandy was thinking the same thing.

"I don't know but I hope they supply cushions. Look at those spines! Damn! I can feel them already and we haven't mounted up yet!"

"Maybe we don't mount them, Pop. Maybe they're just for carrying the equipment and supplies." Beth was hopeful. No such luck.

As the unit approached Heidelberg, it was clear that the roads were impossible for the Recons' armored cars. Mules were flown in to get over the mountains. Sandy thoroughly enjoyed talking about his ass.

The Rainbow Division was in an incredibly mountainous, rugged area with jagged, icy, wooded terrain, much of which was inacces-

110

sible by any vehicle they had. Mules, not donkeys as Beth and Sandy thought they were, could negotiate difficult terrain better than other animals or vehicles. There were motorized vehicles like tanks and jeeps and armored cars, but there were also horses and mules. They were used throughout the war in Europe as cavalry, for which Sandy had trained back in the States, as well as for pulling field artillery and supply trains. Horses played a large role in the German army as well. Ironically, Sandy and his buddies found that both mules and jeeps required pushing and pulling to get across the mountains.

Mules of the 42nd Division

March 7, 1945
My Dearest Darling Wife:
I'm awfully tired tonight. I was on my ass all day today.

"Really, Pop?" snarked Beth.

Maybe I should have explained something before I said that as you may get the wrong impression. I'm sorry, Darling. You see, I am a cowboy now, and I am in the cavalry, so I hope you see why I'm sore and what I meant. We have donkeys and I was on mine from eight o'clock this morning until five o'clock tonight, just getting off long enough to eat dinner, and not being used to it, it really made me sore.

My ass is a nice brown one and he's quite a galloper once he gets going. I haven't given him a name yet but I think I'll name him "Lassie." Don't you feel honored, having an ass named after you? I'm just kidding of course. Tomorrow I only have to ride half a day, thank goodness!! I don't believe I could possibly stand to ride it the whole day.

They're really working you back home, aren't they, Darling? In the bank in the morning and then you have to cook for the family and it just seems as if they can't find enough for you to do. Well, Darling, when I come home I'll make sure that you and I will go away for about a month and not do a thing, just be on a honeymoon. Will you like that? I will.

I never told you about my bed here, did I? Well, we've got straw piled about 2 feet high and we spread our shelter half over it and sleep in our sleeping bags which are really comfortable. It's just like sleeping in a bed.

Well, Darling, I must close for tonight so I'll say goodnight and remind you one more time that I love you very much.

Your loving hubby,
Sandy

After a day of pretending to be King of the Cowboys Roy Rogers on his trusty stead Trigger the mule, Sandy was in pain.

"God, my butt's sore! Even the pad didn't help."

Beth laughed. "I'm not sure but I don't think Jewish boys make very good cowboys."

"Sure they do!" argued Sandy. "What about Eli Graouskay who had a Jewish star on his branding iron? Or Adolphus Sterne who smuggled guns to Sam Houston and fought for Texas independence from Mexico?"

Beth was astonished! She knew Sandy was smart but this ridiculous trivia surprised her. "How do you know about those people, Pop?"

"I don't know. I read a lot."

When Sandy and Beth got back to the command post, Sandy gathered his mail as usual. He was lucky enough to come from a large family, unlike other guys in his unit, so he received mail often. Today was no exception. He was just always surprised that mail could find him so many thousands of miles away from home and on the battle-front.

"Well I'll be damned! Look at this," Sandy said to no one in particular.

"What?" asked Ketch.

"I just got a letter from some gal in St. Louis except it's not to me. It's to her boyfriend who has my same name!"

"You're kidding!"

"No, here it is! I wonder where this guy is and if he's still alive? Maybe I can find him."

"Maybe, Sandy, but not today. We have work to do."

"I know but maybe when we get back home. St. Louis isn't so far from East Liverpool, is it?" (Beth knew that many years later Sandy did indeed find the guy with his same name from St. Louis and they and their wives became great friends.)

Sandy met a young soldier from Pittsburgh, Pennsylvania, while he was guarding the highway. They struck up a conversation and Sandy told the guy that he was from East Liverpool, Ohio.

"No kidding? I know a family in East Liverpool but you prob-ably don't know them."

"Yeah? Who? My dad owns a grocery store and we know pret-ty much everyone in town," said Sandy.

"They have a daughter named Lois and a son Jack. Lois and I had been close friends. I hear she was married a while back. In fact, my mom attended the wedding."

"No kidding! Yeah! I know Lois. Beautiful girl," said Sandy.

"She is. Here. I have a picture of her. I wonder what kind of guy got her, lucky duck."

Beth watched Sandy as he played along with this guy. Then Sandy pulled out the same photo of Lois.

"How'd you get that? It's just like mine? You must know her, too!"

Sandy coolly said, "Well, it's customary for a husband to carry his wife's picture." Sandy was grinning from ear to ear. The two men, who lived only 40 miles apart and were thousands of miles from home, shared lots of stories and fun memories.

Lois Lebman
1943

March 8, 1945
My Dearest Darling Wife;
    I was almost afraid that I would have to write this letter stand-
ing up. I went riding for a half a day today. As long as I was in the
saddle, everything was just fine, but when I got out of it, there I was,
walking like a pregnant woman about eight months along. But the only
way to get used to it is to stick with it. I guess from now on we'll prac-
tically live on these critters, that is, of course, if it doesn't kill me first.

You know, darling, I found out today that there is another man in this army with my same name, believe it or not! I didn't meet him or anything but I got a letter today from his girlfriend in St. Louis. It was to some guy in an ordinance outfit, but the letter's done quite a bit of travelling and it never got to him, but it tracked me down, how, I'll never know. It was mailed on the 12th of Dec. Anyhow, she loves him, whomever he is. Quite a coincidence, don't you think, Darling?

I'm almost twenty now, Darling. I'm really getting old. I can feel old age creeping up on me. I can feel something anyhow, and before long you'll be nineteen. You're fast growing out of your childhood, too, aren't you, Darling?

I'd better close before I get myself into trouble so until tomorrow night, I'll close loving you as always, Darling.

Your loving hubby,
Sandy

On March 9th, horses were added to Sandy's unit for Reconnaissance and patrol duty, so Sandy traded his mule for a proper horse. Sandy and his unit went into enemy lines that day on horseback to fire propaganda leaflets and to get coordinates. Luckily there were no casualties. While morale was higher than usual, the weather was degrading, becoming cloudy, rainy, and cold.

March 10, 1945
My Dearest Darling Wife:

We get a newspaper over here every evening called "The Stars and Stripes." It gives us news of what's going on in the States. Last night I was reading about a flood and I saw East Liverpool mentioned in it. That made me feel pretty good just seeing East Liverpool in print.

I'm not very sore today. I guess I'm gradually getting use to the saddle. We have to ride all afternoon again today but now we've got some real horses to ride, not those asses.

How old is that boy that's moving downstairs from you? You better warn him that you're pretty dangerous for anyone to mess around with, because after a fellow once gets overseas, he gradually gets awfully particular and doesn't take anything from anyone, so word to the wise should be sufficient.

"Pop, why are you so jealous? You are SO going to piss her off."

I'm only kidding, Darling.

"Darned good thing."

Don't take me seriously. I'm very anxious to return to you and endeavor to make you happier than you have ever been before in your life.
I'd better close for now. I'll close loving you and thinking of you every second of every minute of every day.
Your loving hubby,
Sandy

"Pop, what's East Liverpool like?"

"I dunno. It's a small town. Everyone knows everyone else and everyone knows your business."

"Is that okay with you? I think I'd find it stifling."

"It may be but I like it. I have a big family and I like knowing what everyone is doing and where they are. I'm not so good with socializing with people who aren't family but I like the small town feeling."

"What are your parents like?

"I never thought about what they're *like*. I guess my mom is kind of short and her English isn't great. She and my dad are from Poland. His English is pretty good, though. Dad owns a grocery store. And he's big in the synagogue.

"Your handwriting is very nice and your language sounds very educated."

"Thanks. I like to look at nice handwriting and penmanship, so I work hard to make mine look nice. I don't know about educated. It's just East Liverpool schools. But I know I'm smart and I hope to go to college one day. I was supposed to go to Ohio State for pharmacy but I got drafted before I could start school."

"Pharmacy? Really? Cool."

Then Beth asked, "Why are you silent about the hell we're dealing with over here? You write about nicey-nice stuff."

"I don't really have a choice because of the censors. You know that. If they read sensitive material in our letters, they'll cut it out. And

116

I just don't want people back home to worry. This is a pretty darned scary place and they just don't need to know about it."

And you don't talk about it for another 55 years, thought Beth.

As the men approached the German border, the German army fought vigorously even though its days were numbered. Sandy and his men fought fatigue and drowsiness, needing to be ready to attack or fire back at any moment. They worked hard despite the misery, hunger, cold, frustration, loneliness, tension, and fear. They did it because it was their job. And Beth kept asking, *Yes, it's your job but why are you here, really?* There was never another answer other than the job. *When we win, we go home.*

Beth observed that men on the front lines spent a lot of time in foxholes even in the rain and snow and ice. The winter was bitterly cold. Soldiers couldn't take off their boots with wet socks because their feet would freeze. Thousands of men had frostbite and trench-foot. Many lost toenails, toes, and even feet and lower legs because of it.

Beth and Sandy agreed that the German countryside was beautiful but so were the villages, or at least they must have been before they were blown to smithereens.. The Rainbow men turned the towns' taverns into mess halls, regardless of the condition of the buildings. They had hot meals and portable showers nearby. Sandy, Ketch, AJ and Dickie —and Beth—were bunked in a small cabin near the heart of the next little village.

March 11, 1945
My Dearest Darling Wife:

There's a German family that lives next door to us here, and last night they invited myself and the guys over. We had some schnapps and a girl baked a cake for us. She's planning to go to the States when the war is over. They have relatives in Pittsburgh.

I spent the afternoon yesterday and the morning today grooming my horse. He's really a beauty now. He's chestnut brown. I mean she. I think I'll name her "Lassie." I'm serious this time.

If I could get home in time for our first anniversary, Darling, we wouldn't be there to celebrate because I'd elope with you this time and we'd celebrate ourselves, or maybe we'd let our families in on some of it. Wouldn't you like that, Darling?

If you keep gaining weight like you have been, then you'll soon weigh as much as I do. I don't know exactly what I weigh now but I guess it's around 160 lbs. And since you keep gaining weight, that doesn't look so good, does it, Darling?

"Whaaaat? You're here with your life on the line and you're worried about your wife's weight? She's beautiful, and she's a good woman according to you, so who cares if she gains weight?" Beth was furious!

Sandy ignored her.

After we finished riding today, we had to groom our animals, clean their hoofs, and so forth. It's really interesting. Remember I always told you that we'd have to have a couple of horses. Well, I'm more in favor of that now.

I have to close for now, Darling, because I have to get ready to go on guard duty, so until tomorrow night, I remain
Your loving hubby,
Sandy

"Dude, why are you so focused on Lois' weight? It's not really your business, you know."

"Beth, I have a beautiful wife. I want her to stay that way."

"What does beauty have to do with anything, Pop? Isn't it more important that she's wonderful, kind, nice, all that?"

"Yeah, those are important, but with a beautiful wife on my arm, people will think more of me."

"Really, Pop? That's not about beauty. That's insecurity. Yours, not hers." Beth was frustrated.

March 13, 1945
My Dearest Darling Wife:
Remember I told you the other day that I got a letter from someone in St. Louis? Well, the other night, I got a package from his sister in Indianapolis, Indiana. There was some candy and socks, ciga-

rettes, and some other stuff in it. When I opened it I thought that maybe it was one of your packages but I discovered later it wasn't.

The plan to bring wives over here fell through because about 95% of the soldiers are against it while the war is going on. When the war is over, then they can come visit their husbands in the army of occupation. That'll be entirely different.

They put up signs in this town that these people are French citizens in spite of speaking German. They did that because the soldiers here don't trust these people and you can't blame them.

Well, I'm twenty years old now, Darling, and I don't feel a bit over fifty. I'm only kidding as usual. I feel swell, couldn't feel better except that I miss you terribly, Darling, and that's about the worst anyone could feel. But physically, I'm fit as a fiddle.

I dream of you always and no matter what I'm doing or where I am you are always with me. I'd give anything or do anything to put my arms around you and just caress you, Darling. I'll never let go the next time I put my arms around you.

I have to close for tonight, darling. Guard duty calls. I'll close hoping to be with you soon if that's not hoping too much. I'll close loving you always. Oceans of kisses from

Your loving hubby,
Sandy

The bitter wind fiercely struck Sandy's face as the temperature dropped to near freezing. He blew into his hands to try to fight off the cold as he began guard duty. Darkness fell, and Sandy realized how very lonely he was. His wife and family were thousands of miles away and Beth, if she even really existed, was who-knows-where since she seemed to mysteriously come and go. Sandy was bundled up but the bitter cold bit through the fabric and he couldn't stop shivering. At least on guard duty he had plenty of time to think while everything was quiet in the pitch-blackness of the night. Sandy thought about what it meant to be Jewish in a place where Jews are being killed. His heart hurt even though he didn't understand. When his hours of guard duty were over, Sandy quickly made his way to his tent and fell into his makeshift bed for a few hours of sleep. He thought about Beth's questions and about how this war started. Why was he here? He wasn't sure that he knew that...yet.

There are many dates throughout WWII that soldiers will never forget. March 15, 1945, was profound for the Rainbow Division. It was the beginning of the final drive to crush the German army and Nazi Regime, the day the Rainbow Division began the long, difficult and heroic journey which later became known as "Glory Road." The physical and moral fiber of every Rainbow soldier was about to be tested. For the young soldiers, it began their trial and tested their manhood. From that day on they would know death and sorrow and sadness. And yet it was a day of which every Rainbow soldier was proud.

On March 15th, the entire Rainbow Division came together in an attack that lasted until the end of the war. They smashed German defenses in the densely wooded Hardt Mountains and on into Germany. Sandy wondered if they would survive this frightening, exhausting mission. The German army cut trees down across the roads, and there were dangerous land mines all along the way. But the Rainbow kept attacking, crossing the Rhine into Germany, the first U.S. Army division to do so.

Beth, like the soldiers she accompanied, was scared out of her mind. Everyone shook, everyone vomited. There was so much gunfire and screaming. Bullets flew by their heads. Some guy was carrying his own blown-off arm. Guts were hanging out of live and dead bodies. Men hollered for their mothers. Some dragged the dead and wounded by their backpacks. Some were shot up into the air, their faces blown off. Everyone tried to stop the bleeding. Men crossed themselves and kissed their dog tags. Bodies were face down, face up. Chaplains were giving last rites on the battlefield as grenades and bullets landed near them. One guy stepped on a part of a blown up German soldier and tried to clean the guts his boot, but he wasn't able to get rid of the stench of death. Soldiers hid behind the dead carcasses of sheep and cattle as they went through bodies of their buddies to gather dog tags to send to dead soldiers' families.

AJ Jackson, standing right next to Sandy, screamed when he was hit in the stomach by enemy fire. Sandy dropped his weapon and immediately put pressure on the gaping hole while Ketch wiped up his blood. Sandy gave AJ a shot of morphine. Everyone carried vials of morphine in self-injecting tubes. AJ cried out for his mom, then died in Sandy's arms. Sandy, Ketch, Dickie and Beth couldn't see anything around them because they couldn't stop crying. Their friend was dead. Now, for the first time, they had an immediate reason to fight. Their buddy was dead and the krauts would pay.

There was a lull in the fighting though any movement drew heavy fire. The men were able to stop and regroup. Just as they were catching their breath, the German army hit them with a mortar barrage that took a heavy toll of casualties. The mortar fire was intense despite the return fire from Division artillery. The German army knew exactly where the troops were located and systematically blanketed the area with mortar fire. The only safety for the men was to move forward.

Finally, the gunfire was silent. The men advanced through Melk. Beth remembered reading somewhere about Melk. She recalled the sub-camp of the Mauthausen Concentration Camp near Melk. Apparently the purpose of the sub-camp was to use prisoner labor to dig tunnels through the sand-and-quartz hills. It was extermination by labor. Beth noticed that the Melk camp was visible to everyone who passed, including the soldiers. Even the entrance to the crematorium faced the main road. The stench, the atrocities, weren't concealed at all and yet the U.S. soldiers had no idea that they were passing right under Hitler's nose. Beth also saw the beautiful Melk Abby that overlooked the Danube. The dichotomy between the two structures nearly overwhelmed her.

The next day, the German army waited, then attacked again, but the Rainbow, in position at the Rhine, held the bridge. Ketch complained, "We spend most of our time waiting for something: chow, pay, a shower, a bomb, a letter. I can't wait anymore. What will this day bring to us?"

Life, I hope, thought Beth.

Sandy said, " You're probably right, Ketch, but aren't you used to it yet?"

"I'll never get used to this, man. I hope I never do."

The order to move out was issued, and thousands of young men were sent into silent action. The forest was cold, and it was quiet, eerily quiet. The Rainbow Division was a coordinated fighting machine. They moved to the western banks of the Rhine River. The zone of attack was directly through the heart of the heavily forested Hardt Mountains. The river ran parallel to and across the front of the Division, cutting into easily defended areas. Most of the surfaced roads followed the river valleys. The few roads and trails leading to the north were heavily mined. The woods and rocks offered concealment, and the hillcrests provided expansive views. In short, the terrain could not have been more ideal for the defense.

At the end of this forested, mountainous area was the terrifying Siegfried Line, the Nazi West Wall. It was a huge concrete fortification built by the Germans that hid camouflaged forts, minefields, tank obstacles, and gun emplacements in the deep forest. Covered with earth and overgrown with vegetation, the concrete pillboxes formed a secure area 500 yards deep, with a secondary defensive zone to the rear. The Rainbow had to penetrate the Siegfried Line if it intended to move forward into the heart of Germany. German counterattack kept driving the Rainbow Infantry back to the Rhine, but the Rainbow was both powerful and determined against the disorganized but bitterly fighting enemy.

The destroyed Siegfried Line

March 19, 1045
My Dearest Darling Wife:
I've got a chance to write a few words this morning so I stopped everything I was doing to write. We've been pretty much on the go since the push started and I haven't had any time to write. I was in Germany yesterday for the first time. We've been going pretty fast but we haven't been able to catch up with those ___.

If you don't hear from me very much in the next few weeks, Darling, don't worry because it's because I can't write. I'll try to write as often as I can. Until later, Darling, I'll close loving you always.
    Your loving hubby,
    Sandy

The order to attack pillboxes in the Siegfried Line was issued on March 20th. P47 aircraft dive-bombed and strafed the fortification, followed by artillery shelling. Men sat in foxholes and watched the planes and artillery pour their fire into the Siegfried line and prayed that the bombing and the shelling would at least stun the Germans. The artillery shells had little effect on the forts but the bombs put cracks in them and the men inside probably felt every minute would be their last.

Siegfried Line foxhole

Two days later, on March 22nd, between the intensity of the infantry and the P47 dive-bombing the forts, the Rhine was crossed near Worms, a German city on the western bank of the Rhine a few miles north of Mannheim and 25 miles south of Mainz. It was one of the last towns in the area that remained under German control. The Americans entered the city and established a bridgehead. There was only isolated resistance, but Worms had already been heavily damaged.

As the troops began crossing the Rhine into Germany, Sandy said, "This is the first crossing of the Rhine by an invading army since Napoleon Bonaparte in 1813."

Beth looked at Sandy in surprise. "How do you know that?"

"I dunno. It's one of those tidbits I remember from my history class. Kind of like the Norman invasion of Britain in 1066."

The German army was no longer surprised as more American troops crossed the Rhine. The invasion into Germany was in full swing. Within three days U.S. troops approached Frankfurt and captured intact bridges as German defenses began to fall apart. Sandy and the Recons led the way. If they ran into a roadblock or enemy fire or snipers in houses, the tanks would blast the resistance mercilessly, and villages and towns were reduced to rubble. Civilians were given two hours to vacate their homes so the soldiers could temporarily move in.

March 25, 1945
My Very Dearest Darling Wife:

Here I am again after not writing for many days. We're resting for a few days now because we're just sitting here not doing a thing. I don't mind that at all though. There are still lots of krauts in these hills because every once in a while a few will come down waving a white flag.

I haven't been able to answer all your letters that I received during the push because I had to destroy them as soon as I read them, because in case of capture we didn't want the jerries to get them but I got one from you this morning. It was written on my birthday and I was so glad to hear that all of you had celebrated for me and had a good time, because, believe me, we're not having any fun over here. I haven't even shaved since the push started but I think I'll shave today. That is all except my moustache. It's got a pretty good start this time so I think I'll let it grow for a while.

I'm sorry I used that vulgar word when I was telling you of our donkey, Darling. I promise never to do it again. I hope you'll forgive me. As for the animals, we haven't got them any more. When we started this push we left them behind and as far as I'm concerned I hope I never see them again.

Things have really been different since we entered Germany. You don't see those smiling faces and hands waving. Now you see tears and you have to watch these civilians closely and treat them as if they were jerries. The people in Germany, though, seem to have more than did those in France. They seem to live a better life, but we'll fix that up.

[two lines censored]

I'll have to close now, Darling, because I have to get cleaned up and have some things to do before we get another order to move on. I'll try to write again tomorrow, Darling.

Your loving hubby,
Sandy

"Pop, why do you use the terms *kraut* and *jerries*?" Beth was concerned about scapegoating, about using names to dehumanize people to justify bullying and worse. She had thought about this a few weeks ago but now Sandy's letter brought the thought back to her.

"Because that's what they are. They're not human. They're not people I want to know. I don't like them, don't respect them, and they're scum."

"I guess it's easier to shoot at people who are probably not too different from yourself in age and dreams and family if you don't think they're human," said Beth.

"I don't care, Beth. They're the enemy and I'm here to kill them. That's what Uncle Sam says I have to do, so I do it."

Again Beth wondered *is this why you're here? To kill human beings because the government says you have to?"*

March 26, 1945
Somewhere in Germany
My Dearest Darling Wife:

I can't express my thanks enough for the lovely watch I got. It was swell. I just can't find the words in which to express my feelings. I believe you know how I feel, Darling, although I wish you wouldn't have gotten it because you know how sensitive I am in getting a gift from you, because it makes me feel so cheap.

You asked about a couple of the abbreviations we use here. O.P. means Observation Post. It's a point from which you observe enemy action. A CP is a Command Post where the command element is.

Next week is Pesach (Passover), Darling, so I guess it would just be fitting and proper for me to wish you a very happy Pesach.

I'll have to close for now, my love. Until tomorrow I'll close loving you with all my heart and thank you once again for the lovely watch.

Your loving hubby
Sandy

On March 26, in the town of Dahn, all battalions gathered in an assembly area for reorganization and to consolidate units. All vehicles and equipment were inspected, repaired, and maintained. The men turned in their winter clothing because the weather was getting warmer.

It was also a time for celebration. The Allies knew that they were winning and that the German army was severely disabled. They held an awards ceremony and implanted flags from each of the 48 States on German soil. They also gave out Purple Heart medals to those who had been wounded. Sandy received two Purple Hearts that day.

Flags of the 48 States parade for the first time in Germany

U.S. Flag Parade, March 26, 1946, Dahn, Germany

General Harry Collins read a letter of commendation to the gathered assembly.

APO 411, U.S. Army
26 March 1945
SUBJECT: Commendation
TO: The Infantry

1. These outstanding combat successes accomplished by the Infantry in the Division's recent operation are worthy of high praise, and I take this opportunity to congratulate and commend you upon your accomplishments and a job well done.

2. In a large measure, this success can be attributed to the active patrolling performed on our first defensive position, and the determination on the part of officers and men to carry through. The active patrolling performed on our first defensive position was done primarily to give our troops the confidence that they could close with and defeat the enemy, and secondarily to determine enemy dispositions both as to personnel and mines, and to determine the weak spots in his defensive position. Both were successful. Every officer and man on every patrol that accomplished its mission, both combat and Reconnaissance patrols, enabled this Division to drive through the soft spots in the enemy position and accomplish this remarkably successful operation with the absolute minimum of casualties. To those who were members of these successful patrols and to those who made sound tactical use of this information and drove through with esprit and the will-to-do, I give my heartfelt thanks and congratulations. Through their efforts the Division has accomplished an outstanding job which has cost the enemy severely in prisoners, killed and wounded and materiel and at the same time saving thousands of lives of our own Rainbowers.

3. Another chapter has been written in our history, and I know we will continue to add success after success in future operations in the European Theatre. Again, congratulations and nice going!

HARRY J. COLLINS
Major General, U.S. Army

March 27, 1945
Somewhere in Germany
My Dearest Darling Wife:
   I can hardly wait until the 16th of April so that I can wear the watch. I don't want to put it on until then because I don't think it's right, but it's pretty hard for me to wait until then. Every time I look at it, I think it's nice and I just want to put it on, but I'll wait until our anniversary.
   We've been having awful weather the past couple of days. Its been raining and that makes the day awful dull and dreary, and our sleeping bags get all wet. It's a miserable feeling.
   This morning when we got up they told us to go take a shower. I was glad to take a shower but it was too early in the day and it was cold. But the quartermaster put up a shower tent and so we got to take a shower.
   Since I can't think of anything else to write, Darling, I'll close for now. Remaining the one that loves you most.
   Your loving hubby,
   Sandy

   Sandy met a couple of Jewish guys from another unit while in Dahn.

   "Hey, Sandy. You going to the Passover thing tonight?" asked Bernie Horwitz.

   "Yeah. Wouldn't miss it," answered Sandy. *Good,* thought Beth. *I want to go, too.*

   "Are your family Seders traditional?"

   "If that means hours of stories and prayers and food, they sure are. I like it. I enjoy listening to my Dad sit at the head of the table with my sisters and brother all around and my Mom's cooking. It's special to me so I'm glad they're doing this even if it's a few days early," Sandy shared.

   "I like the story of the Jews' exodus from Egypt. It's the story of freedom. Kind of fitting for this place, for sure. And I like the prayers, especially the ones that pray for our beloved dead," said Horwitz.

   "I think this year we need to pray for our beloved alive...like ourselves," laughed Sandy.

   "I just heard that General Collin's had a *Haggadah* printed just for us," said Harvey Lazar.

"Really?" ask Sandy. "I'm kind of surprised. When did he even have time to do it?"

"I don't think he personally did it. But he gave Rabbi Bohnen permission to hold the Seder for us. And he gave all of us Jewish soldiers permission to leave our units to attend. Impressive!" said Lazar.

Rabbi Bohnen found a fairly undamaged auditorium in a schoolhouse in Dahn, Germany. He got some of the Nazi prisoners to clean it while he composed a *Haggadah* from some Hebrew prayer books. He had it printed on the Division newsletter printer.

"I heard that the printers used Nazi flags to clean the presses then made a hundred copies," offered Lazar.

Though Passover wasn't until April 5th, the Seder was held on March 28, 1945, because of the lull in the fighting. It was the first Passover Seder to be held in Germany since the Nazis came to power, and the *Haggadah* was likely the first Hebrew religious work printed in Germany since the rise of Hitler. Many Jewish soldiers and even some Christians attended, as did some German civilians. The windows of the auditorium were opened so that people could watch this ceremony that celebrated freedom.

Sandy asked, "Did you guys know that Jewish athletes were expelled from all German sports? And three Jewish American runners were not allowed to compete in the 1936 Olympics?"

None of the men knew that. And none were yet knowledgeable about the Holocaust and the extermination of the Jews. They still didn't know why they were fighting this war.

"Yeah, and the Nazis were very embarrassed when that Negro runner Jesse Owens beat the white Germans with four gold medals, more than anyone else ever got that year."

"No shit!" exclaimed Horwitz.

"Good for him!" agreed Lazar.

Dickie, Ketch, and Beth listened. They didn't know, either.

March 29, 1945
My Dearest Darling Wife:
Tonight I'm going to go to Passover service. I know it's a little early but I guess they're going to have it while we can because when

we leave here we probably won't be able to have any, and it's hard to tell when we'll start out again which I doubt will be very long from now.

The Rainbow Division made history again yesterday, Darling, at a ceremony in which the general awarded some medals. They had flags from all forty-eight states flying. It's the first time that all forty-eight state flags have been flown in Germany.

The M.P.s are on the ball. When someone even talks to some girl or woman, they're really right there behind them and pick them up. Although I don't see why anyone would want to talk to any German person because in my estimation they're just as bad as the jerries.

I guess I have to close for now, Darling, and get washed and cleaned up before I go to services. So until tomorrow, I'll close by loving you with all my heart.

Your loving hubby,
Sandy

Rainbow *Haggadah*, Dahn, Germany

Thunderstorms and snowy rain ruled the day on March 29th. Fighting had subsided as the soldiers rested in Dahn on their trek across Germany. Though Passover wasn't for another couple of days, the Seder, the Passover dinner that celebrates the freedom of the Jews from Egypt, was held that day, in the Nazi Meeting Hall on Adolph Hitler Street No. 29. Such irony!

Sandy invited Ketch and Dickie to go with him to the Seder. The Jewish soldiers thought of their families back home. As Sandy and the men talked more about Passover and their families, Beth listened intently. She sure didn't learn any of this in her history classes at school or even in her home. The Seder fascinated her. This is her history, too, and she wanted to know more.

To everyone's amazement, dozens of Jewish civilians who had been in hiding also attended the Seder, crying for joy but also with pain for the loss of their loved ones. For the first time in nearly 15 years, they were free to celebrate Passover openly. The service was conducted by the division's Jewish chaplain, Rabbi Eli A. Bohnen and Eli Heimberg, both of whom created the Rainbow *Haggadah*. The 42nd Infantry Rainbow Division commander told the men, "You celebrate today in Germany, in the land in which Hitler said no Passover would be celebrated for at least a thousand years. Next year may you celebrate in Jerusalem."

At the Seder

Passover is about freedom. The soldiers, and Beth, suddenly realized that they were creating freedom for people in Germany by destroying the Nazi regime. Amen.

March 29, 1945
Somewhere in Germany
My Dearest Darling Wife:
   I have to get up at 2 AM. Our mission is to guard the Division C.P. There's nothing to it except that we have to be on duty all the time, but I'd rather be doing that than some other things I can think of.
   Last night I attended Passover services and it was really quite an affair that's really something for the history books. I wrote Mom and Dad about the whole thing, Darling, so you can read their letter rather than have me write the same thing.
   Yesterday the Rainbow band was here and played quite a few pieces. You'd be surprised how homesick music can make you, especially when they played "It had to be you." I almost went AWOL but then I started thinking it over and decided that you wouldn't like that very much so I stayed. It doesn't take a heck of lot to make you homesick over here.
   It's still raining. Boy, how I hate that when it starts raining over here. It just keeps pouring for about two weeks at a time and then we have some nice weather, and then it starts again. I hope you're having nicer weather than this at home, Darling, so that you can go out and enjoy yourself a little.
   We get a chance to take another shower today so I have to take advantage of that. There's nothing I like better than to take a shower. When we build our home, Darling, remind me to have a shower installed, will you?
   I have to close for now, Darling. I love you very much and wish that those thousands of miles of water would dry up so we could walk to each other. I miss you terribly. So until later, I remain
      Your loving hubby,
      Sandy

A showdown inspection was held the next day. Officers searched the soldiers for "souvenirs" they may have taken from German soldiers' bodies or from buildings in Dahn and the towns in which they'd already fought and vacated.

"You got anything, Sandy?" asked Ketch.

"Heck, yeah! I got a Luger off one of the dead krauts. It's a beaut. Semi-automatic. If I had ammo for it, I'd use it to kill more of 'em." Sandy boasted, showing the pistol to Ketch and the others. "Did you guys get anything?"

"Yeah, I found one of those little wooden land mine boxes, but the inspectors took it from me. I was able to keep a belt, though. See?" Ketch showed the guys his prize: a Nazi military uniform belt with a steel buckle. The men examined it. They saw that the surface was pebbled and had two ropes, one inside the other, that formed a circle in the center. An eagle with retracted wings in the center of the inner circle was clutching a swastika. Ironically, in the upper half of the circle were the words "GOTT MIT UNS," *God with us. Really?,* thought Beth. *God? I think God forgot about Germany.*

Along with the searches, soldiers were also reminded of the non-fraternization rules, forbidding social contact with German civilians. But for many of the men, it was too late. Some soldiers, like Sandy, sent their pay home to their wives, but others spent their money on the women in Dahn.

Beth watched the young soldiers do everything they could, conscious and unconscious, to deal with the homesickness, the pain, and the loneliness that shrouded them. It was easy to see the physical wounds, of course, but the invisible emotional wounds were every bit as painful. The soldiers sought distractions to escape their destructive reality. Many of their remedies were sexual: pornography, lewd humor about women, lies about their conquests at home. Profanity peppered their conversations. Alcohol distracted them from the terrifying images of blown-up bodies and bloody fragments. Alcohol was abundant and cheap and helped to blot out the terror, the screams, the noise of the bullets and bombs, the death and destruction. Temptations were plentiful and irresistible. The men headed to the women in town. Sandy didn't go with the others. He had guard duty that night.

The men returned, laughing about the large, mostly blown-up building in the public square. "What a dump!" exclaimed Ketch. "And those dames were awful. Efficient but awful."

"Sounds like you guys had a good time," said Sandy, "but aren't you worried about what your wives will think? What if you get a disease?"

"That's what the medicine's for! I don't care. I needed to get laid, Sandy. Anyway, who's gonna tell my wife? Not me!" laughed one of the men.

A night on the town

Another guy thought about the evening. "You know," he began, "it was all pretty sad. I mean, I'm glad I got off and all but I felt really sorry for those girls. They just sat next to each other with their backs up against the wall. They were wearing plain old everyday clothes that were pretty ragged, nothing sexy at all. I don't think they were the professional types, you know what I mean? They just looked like ordinary housewives."

Remorse? thought Beth. *Was this guy feeling remorse? That would be a first in this crowd!* Beth knew that the German women needed money to care for what was left of their families. There was no other work, no other people in their lives to whom they could turn for support. It was up to these women to offer themselves in exchange for, well, survival. These women were family providers, doing a job in silence. Beth knew the scene: next to each woman was a small pile of coins. If a soldier added a coin to the collection, he could have sex with her in this very public setting. The soldier's buddies held up a sheet for some privacy while the soldier stood in front of the women, getting jerked or sucked off. Then the soldier went back to his buddies to brag about the conquest. *Pathetic*, thought Beth.

A couple of the guys joined the conversation. One said, "I missed that building. There's an open-air bordello not too far from here. We went over there. The dames were hot and wild and crazy for us!"

Beth doubted that statement. The women were traumatized and emaciated, prostituting themselves in exchange for survival. Most of the women had gonorrhea. The men fornicated with wild abandon, and the gonorrhea rate among them rose dramatically. Regardless, it was a different time. The men were scared. They lived for the moment because they didn't know if they had a future, so they grabbed every little slice of happiness, even if it meant dealing with a case of the clap.

"I don't know, fellas," pondered on of the older soldiers. "Maybe this wasn't a good idea but, God, I needed it. I can't wait 'til I can hold a dame in my arms on U.S. soil and not have to pay her, but I'm okay with this for now."

Beth could understand the men getting all wound up. What she simply could not stomach was the ways in which the soldiers treated the local people, especially the women, in Dahn and in the other towns in which they had fought. She knew that the young girls in town were very sweet to Sandy, as he was to them, but she sometimes questioned his motives. She knew he was very lonely, but she trusted his level of commitment to his wife. She also knew that the young girls and old women who remained in the towns through which soldiers of every army marched, were repeatedly raped and abused. In Dahn, as the men debauched and partied, Beth thought about the children. More than ever, she wanted to know their stories.

Soldiers could keep very little with them on the battlefield. Photographs from home were the most precious things they had. They kept them as safe as possible, usually stuffing them into their helmets. Sandy did the same with pictures of Lois, and he also had her photo in his new M8 armored car.

The M8, Sandy's third, was assigned to him in Dahn so that he and his crew could continue to conduct their Reconnaissance work into the heart of Germany. This new M8, made by Ford, was fitted with an M6 rifle, a Browning machine gun in the turret, and a Browning anti-aircraft gun. Even Beth liked the shiny new M8 and felt a bit safer in it as they prepared to move forward.

The last day of March 1945, was Easter Sunday, and the Infantry began to move forward. There was no longer an organized German front line, just isolated resistance in the villages. Dazed and shaken German prisoners were beginning to arrive in increasing numbers.

Beth needed a break from the fighting, and she wanted to know more about the children. She sent a message to the other avatars, Ludvig and Kate, to meet her in Mainz.

12.

THE CHILDREN

Mainz, Germany is a port town where the Rhine and the Main rivers meet. Mainz was the home of Johannes Gutenberg, born in 1395, who created the first printed books using metal movable type. Gutenberg's first book from movable type was the *Forty-Two-Line Bible*, completed in 1455. Gutenberg died in Mainz in 1468.

During World War II, over 80 percent of Mainz' center, including most of the historic buildings, were destroyed. The Nazi flag flew throughout the city while the Bishop of Mainz, Albert Stohr, secretly helped Jews escape from Germany. Mainz was captured by the U.S. Army under Patton in late March of 1945 and used as a gateway for entrance into the heartland of Germany. Though Mainz was one of the heaviest bombed out cities of World War II, it was an important port and by mid-April soldiers from every allied nation and Russia had been through it.

———————————

The three avatars, Ludvig from Germany, Kate from Canada, and Beth met at the base of the Eisenturm Tower which was built in 1240 as a watchtower and gateway into the city. As they walked through the town, they saw rubbled buildings and twisted metal, and they could smell the acridity of the bombings. They wondered if and where they'd find young people with whom to talk. It didn't take long.

Three girls were scavenging for food. When the avatars saw them, Beth and Kate immediately offered them some K-ration food packs while Ludvig introduced himself in German.

"Please, don't be afraid. We come as friends. Please, here, we have food for you."

The girls looked frightened but they took the food, and they didn't run away. Ludvig continued in German. "I am Ludvig and this is Kate and Beth. We're here from another time to learn about what's happening here." He offered more food.

"What are your names?" asked Beth.

The girl who seemed to be the oldest identified herself and the others. "I'm Karla. This is my sister, Maria, and this is our cousin Letta."

"How old are you?" asked Kate. Karla and Letta were 16. Maria was 14.

"Where is your family?" asked Ludvig.

"Gone," said Karla without emotion. "There's no one left from our family but us."

"All dead," said Maria. "May we have more?" she asked as she looked at the bags the avatars carried. They gave all of it to the three girls.

They could hear the low steady drone of bombers in the distance. Letta said, "We are waiting to die, listening to the engine sounds. They'll come back to bomb again though there's nothing left here. Just us."

Beth asked, "What happened here? What did you see?" The avatars were not prepared to hear the unimaginable lives of the three girls.

Children in a blown-up German town

Karla began. "Our family home had been hit by many fire-bombs in the early years of the war. The men stood on the roofs of the houses during the bombing raids and shoveled the small firebombs into a sandbox they put on the roof. The sandbox allowed the firebombs to burn out harmlessly. But later the planes would drop a mixture of bigger bombs with the firebombs. The bombs ripped open the roof of the houses and then the firebombs set the buildings on fire. We couldn't defend against these."

"Did you know what was happening? Did you know about the war?" asked Kate.

"Yes. Of course," said Letta. "We had a radio. It was a *volksempfänger*, a 'peoples radio' with a dial to tune into different stations. We assembled in the cellar with other families when the air raids started. The sirens would howl, and we'd go down into the cellar and wait for the bombs to fall. The steps of the cellar were so steep. The ground shook and lights flickered. We sat on wooden benches along rough concrete walls of the small room, all piled in so tight. It felt like a tomb."

Karla said, "Sometimes I felt claustrophobic because of so many nights in overcrowded area shelters, in darkness and constant fear of possibly getting buried alive."

Maria added, "During the daytime there were American bombers and during the nighttime they were British. The British targeted neighborhoods. The Americans targeted the industrial area. The Russians just targeted people. But that made little difference for us. We were targets for everyone. Our families lived just a few blocks away from a factory that the Americans constantly targeted. Little did they know it was just an abandoned chocolate factory."

"But soon," said Letta, "the radio would give an all clear signal, and our family would return to our rooms upstairs to continue our night or our day. We tried to live normally even though the walls of our house were gone and food was scarce. Every day was bad news. We would watch the airplanes fly overhead, filling the sky like locusts. Then looting began. Soldiers smashed windows of the jewelry store and pocketed everything. They broke into a safe in the German headquarters and took several hundred thousand marks."

Karla said, "In January a detonation bomb hit our house and blew the foundation apart causing most of the house to collapse. But four rooms were left standing though the walls were open. The bomb that hit our house was probably destined for the bridge over on the Rhine, just five blocks away. That bridge was soon blown apart anyway and it fell into the river. That stopped trains from crossing the river, and the rubble blocked all the shipping traffic on the Rhine. That day was a great disaster and a devastating blow to Germany and to our families."

The avatars noticed that rubble at least six feet high covered the street. The rubble used to be houses. The thousands of inhabitants who lived there at the beginning of the war were gone.

Karla continued, "The bombing was so intense. Our homes are gone. We live in the mess now, making shelters as we can. We stood in ration lines when there was food to give out. We hoped along with other women and girls that the Americans would get here before the Russians because the Soviet troops have a fondness for rape." Her voice quieted and slowly she said. "But that didn't happen. We were brutalized."

Letta said, "Our fear of sexual attack was great. It runs through the city like a plague. Many of our friends committed suicide after the Russians were here. I thought about it but my cousins needed me."

Maria said, "We heard about an orphanage in Berlin, the Haus Dehlem, which was also a maternity hospital. The Russian soldiers went there and repeatedly raped pregnant women and women who had just given birth. These were not isolated incidents. Too many women and girls—who knows how many? —were raped in Germany."

Karla said, "Just last month, a friend of our mother told us that the Soviets entered Danzig and raped her fifteen-year-old niece seven times and her twenty-two-year-old sister fifteen times. A Soviet officer told a group of women to seek safety in the Cathedral there. Once the women were securely locked inside, those beasts raped all of them, some more than thirty times, even eight-year-old girls! They shot the little boys who tried to shield their mothers!"

The avatars had no words. Tears covered their faces.

———————————

Beth had heard from the men in Sandy's unit that they were told by their commanding officers to "teach these Germans a lesson, and have a wonderful time." For the American and British troops, open rape was not as common as among the Soviets. The Soviets raped any female of any age from infants to grandmothers. If a German man or woman killed a Russian soldier for anything including rape, 50 Germans were killed for each incident. But for U.S. troops, having that "wonderful time" depended on the cooperation of the German women. From the starving and the homeless, sexual "cooperation" could be bought for a few pennies or a mouthful of food. Regardless, both the

U.S. and British troops did their share of looting and raping.

————————————

Kate asked, "What do you do now? What do you do each day?"

Maria said, "We try to help the people who survive and then bury the dead which is hard to do when the ground is still frozen from winter. We're not strong enough to break the iced-over land. There are no men in our town. Men or boys. It's just us and the older women right now."

Karla said, "Our parents were hanged because our uncle refused to join the army. The Nazis kill as many German people as Jews, it seems, only they take the Jews away, and they leave Germans in town to hang and rot as a warning to others. We live without feelings. I just can't think about yesterday or tomorrow. This moment is all we have. When does one get used to this?"

Letta said, "When planes were coming near, the sirens would sound both high and low pitches, and that meant full alert. People would run with their suitcases and baby carriages to the nearest bunkers. Street car brakes screeched in an attempt to stop the trolley in its tracks. People would run home to grab gas masks and steel helmets. We were so scared that we couldn't even scream while bombs were whistling outside. We could feel the ground roll, and we could hear the crashes. And then we could smell the smoke..." She broke off, tears running down her face

Maria added, "Our house is a pile of broken bricks. We haven't counted all the dead yet. They are under all the rubble."

Beth remembered hearing about "earthquake" bombs. When an earthquake bomb hits, all that's left is cement powder, small pieces of clothing, body parts, and lots of blood. To escape the madness of these bombs, some people run into the forest, if they can get there in time, which seemed to be one of the safer places.

"I saw people killed by falling bricks and heard the screams of others dying in the fire. I dragged my best friend Hilde from a burning building. She died in my arms." Letta was sobbing now.

"And the following night," added Karla, "a section of town ceased to exist after the British did a, what to call it. It was like a spray of bombs across the town."

"Carpet bombing," said Beth.

"Yes, carpet bombing," said Karla. "I was in the cellar and tried to get underneath an old couch. I thought if the building collapsed the springs of the couch would give some airspace in which to breath." Karla took a breath. "After the all-clear from the air raid, we left the cellar. It was a beautiful day, but we couldn't see the sun because everything was greenish with burning cloth and paper floating through the air. It was dark in the middle of the day. The first thought that came to my mind was that the British used poison gas. Later we learned that the Americans had bombed a chemical factory across the canal. In our house, the windows were gone. I was glad to be alive."

Maria said, "Many of the children remained in the cellars in makeshift beds for days at a time. Nervous disorders became quite common. It was shocking to get out on the street after the all-clear following a daytime raid to see a big empty space where before there had been a large apartment building. The site of the mangled bodies of our neighbors, body parts dangling from the rain-gutters, affected all of us."

"We live in a twilight zone between life and death," said Karla. "And any German citizen who waves the white flag of surrender faces death by firing squad or hanging to show that Germany is not a quitter. The German soldiers are as brutal as the Russians sometimes. For example, my ration of one piece of bread fell from my shaking hand. Before I could pick it up, a boot crushed down on the slice, pushing it deeper into the mud. Through my tears, I saw the black silhouette of a German officer. I waited for him to move off of my bread. When he did, I grabbed the bread from the mud and pressed it against my dress to get rid of the worst of the filth."

Beth's stomach turned.

Kate asked, " What was it like before the actual war started? What was life in Mainz like for you and for your Jewish friends?"

Letta started, "People in our town were proud but where were all the proud folks when the Nazis descended on the town leaders with violence and imprisonment? People retreated into what they thought was the safety of their homes and stayed quiet with their heads in the sand trying not to provoke. Seemingly good Germans changed their allegiance to the Hitler party because they hoped things would get better. This didn't save them from trouble, though. The threat of winding up in a concentration camp was enough to bend the will of the strongest. Few knew the full extent of the enormity of the horrors that lie ahead. Everyone was legally responsible for everyone else's compliance. You couldn't trust anybody. Children denounced their parents. Businessmen denounced competitors. Employees denounced rivals. Treachery was everywhere. No wonder we were fearful and suspicious. It was demoralizing. Much to our disgrace, too many Germans tacitly supported the Nazis madness, fearful for their own lives and the loss of their loved ones."

Beth knew that the barbarism of the Nazis towards their own people was terrible. There were waves of arrests, gruesome torture, and death sentences carried out in public. A favorite form of death was slow strangling while victims were suspended by piano wire from meat hooks taken from butcher shops and slaughterhouses. Relatives and friends of suspects were sent to concentration camps where many died. There wasn't much of a unified resistance movement in Germany. When discovered, all those who secretly worked against the Third Reich were charged with high treason and killed.

Karla continued, "If the attacks on our town weren't enough, this was one of the coldest winters ever. We wear many layers of anything we can find, socks, coats, shawls, scarves because we have no fuel. There's no food, so we scavenge. Our friends died in great numbers from starvation. People forage for food like animals. It's been so long since we've had anything to eat, and we thank you for this food. We'll share it with the others. Maybe we will find a few rotten vegetables, some beans, maybe a slice of cheese. We had a food allowance, but it's gone. We can't concentrate on empty stomachs, and with so much rotten food, my stomach is often upset. Some people are now eating horses and cats and dogs and even rats. Soup is made from sawdust. And we can't bathe because there's very little water and no soap."

Letta said, "We're grateful for all this food you give us. Food is incredibly scarce and therefore an obsession. Next to the constant worries about food is the fight against the cold. The winter was so cold, and we had so little clothing." She added, "We can get food from people at the train, but we have to be careful. If we get milk, we have to beware the dirty water they use to thin it down. They throw dead rats into the mincer to make mincemeat. And worms infest the bread."

Kate asked, "How do you pay for the food if you're able to get it?"

The three girls looked at one another, embarrassed by the only answer they had. "We trade our bodies for it," whispered Maria. The avatars put their arms around the girls. They cried together.

After a while, Beth gently asked, "Why did people follow Hitler and the Nazis?" She was thinking of the 2016 political campaign for the U.S. presidency and the frenzy over several radical candidates.

Karla said, "It wasn't always like that. There used to be street gangs of teenagers in Cologne who beat up Nazi Youth. The Gestapo called them Edelweiss Pirates. They did everything the Nazis hated like listen to jazz and befriend Jewish youth. In Essen, the Farhtenstenze gang organized secret camping trips to the mountains and generally broke the rules. They became bolder, so both the Hitler Youth and the Gestapo went after them. They were tortured and hanged where everyone could see them."

Letta said, "Every day at school we had to stand up, thrust out our arms, and shout Heil Hitler. Once a week we had to go to the auditorium to listen to a propaganda speech by Hitler. There was no way to avoid it."

The importance of state authority was so well drilled into young people's heads that some turned their parents in to the authorities for expressing views at odds with the official Nazi political line. Children were forced to join a branch of the Hitler Youth program depending on their age. Each member of the Hitler Youth, all boys, had to swear an oath to Hitler personally, not to Germany. Girls had to join the BDM.

Karla said, "The BDM is the League of German girls, the Bund Deutscher Madel. Boys said the BDM stood for bubi druck mir (baby do me)." Male youth were granted autonomy from parents and allowed liberal relations with girls their own age.

Maria said, "Some of the young German women who cause trouble are sent to Lesensborn houses to make babies with Nazi soldiers. The babies are cared for in maternity houses, not with the birth mother who has to make more babies."

Adolescents were drawn to the authoritarian nature of the Nazi regime and its ideology of the survival of the fittest. They had an incredible sense of superiority. Many were inducted into the Hitler Youth at very young ages and taught racial hatred and warfare. By 1939, all adolescent boys from age eight to eighteen were obligated to be in the Hitler Youth. By then the suicide rate among German university students was three times as high as in the general population. In addition, over 6,000 boys suspected of homosexual tendencies were expelled

144

and sent to work camps.

Children were sent to live with Nazi families and found it difficult to interact with their birth parents. Beth knew that recently the German army started calling up the very young of the Hitler Youth as soldiers. In fact, some 4500 boys were killed in the last battle of Berlin. The boys had little fighting experience and were quickly destroyed. No Hitler Youth war games prepared the young soldiers for the death and destruction they experienced daily.

The German women were lonely and felt deserted. Karla stated, "The pool of marriage prospects dried up. Soldiers were either missing or disfigured or dead." She added that "the only thing that kept me sane was going to school, but now there is no school. Jewish people were taken away to be killed, then German men and boys were taken away to fight. All that was left in town were young girls, some women, and old people over the age of 60. Now, though, almost all are gone."

Maria continued, "We knew we were facing something terrible, but we couldn't do anything about it. It feels like a dream that you're trying to escape from, some unseen horror, but your screams are silent. I remember seeing bodies loaded onto trucks and taken to the cemetery after the bombs fell. Now people have lice, and there is typhus. I know that our survival depends on keeping as clean as we can as well as doing whatever we must do keep the bombs from dropping on our heads." The other two girls agreed.

Beth noticed Letta scratching at her arms. "My body always itches. Rats and bugs are everywhere, and we all have lice." Then in a childlike voice, Letta smiled for the first time and said, "But we're happy to get chocolates from the American soldiers."

Ludvig asked if the girls had Jewish friends.

"Yes, of course, but friend after friend and their families disappeared into the night."

"Why? Do you know?" asked Kate.

"Either they were accused of being intellectuals, or they questioned what was happening, or they had money. My friend's family had a shop. The windows were broken and the army took everything that was in it. And then they set the shop on fire," explained Letta.

Maria added, "One of my Jewish friends told me that she was afraid every day and that each day brought new miseries for her family. They were banned from public transportation, couldn't participate in sports or swim in the public pool or play tennis or hockey. There was a sign at the ice rink that said that Jews and dogs were not permitted. Park benches were painted yellow for Jews and green for Germans. They couldn't even go to the movies."

Karla said, "We were told that Jews were evil and that the war was their fault. I didn't believe that. I had many good Jewish friends. I knew that wasn't true. But the Nazis arrested Jews on the streets, in cafés, in restaurants, even in their homes. And they were gone without a trace."

Maria offered, "Anti-Semitism was alive and well in Germany long before Hitler came to power. We were all taught in church that Jews had killed Jesus. And Jews must be good investors because they had money when no one else did. At least that's what we were told, but we didn't believe the bad stuff, right, Karla?" Karla and Letta both agreed.

"Selling the idea that the Jews were to blame for all of Germany's problems was just not that difficult. We were told that Jews are inferior, worse than Russians or Poles, with no conscience and no interest in anything but money and diamonds. They were evil and conniving. Hitler made Jews the common enemy," added Karla.

Letta said, "My friends sometimes disappeared in the middle of the night, there one day, gone the next. Once I saw friends in a line at a cattle car train. They went into one car and their luggage went into another. The luggage car was uncoupled from the first car, so the luggage wasn't going with them. I tried to believe that my friends were simply being resettled, that nothing bad happened to them. But we hear what others say, that our Jewish friends are dead."

Maria added, "I watched German soldiers mock my Jewish friends, laugh at them, strike them with whips and send them marching down the road in the deep snow. I saw people lined up carrying only bags and dragging their children. I saw one German soldier hold a child by its feet and smash its head into a wall. He said it was too skinny to be made into soup." She added with such sadness, "I sneaked over to the Jewish quarter. It was empty. Everyone was gone."

Karla said, "We heard later that the trains were going to Theresienstadt, Czechoslovakia. Something very bad is happening there." The avatars knew that there was a concentration camp in Theresienstadt.

Beth asked, "Did you see Jewish people wearing yellow Stars of David on their clothing?"

The three girls nodded. Karla explained, "Every Jewish person we knew, even babies, had to wear the yellow star with the word *Juden* (Jew) on it. They had to wear it on the left side of their clothing so any German could easily see it. My friend Rebecca said the patch meant she was no longer a human being. She and all the others were subjected to constant humiliation, and could be stopped and searched any time and any place. The Star of David served as a badge of shame. Rebecca told me she had been robbed of her freedom. Everything is forbidden, and punishment for everything is death. And I couldn't do anything to help." Karla was crying once again.

Kate and Beth wrapped their arms around Karla. Beth said softly, "You're remembering Rebecca now. She will continue on in your heart, in the heart of her friend."

Beth knew that in towns and villages, the ghettos usually consisted of just a few streets, demarcated by barbed wire. Ghettos isolated Jews by separating Jewish communities from non-Jewish populations and from each other. The Germans established at least 1000 ghettos. Viewing the Jews as a racial threat and an enemy, the Germans incarcerated them as a security measure. The first ghetto was in Poland in October 1939. With the implementation of the Final Solution—the planned execution of all European Jews, beginning in late 1941— Germans systematically destroyed the ghettos. Germans either shot ghetto residents in mass graves located near the ghettos, or deported them, usually by train, to the killing centers—the concentration camps—where they were murdered.

Life in the ghetto was unbearable. Overcrowding was common. Plumbing broke down so human waste was thrown into the streets along with the garbage. Contagious diseases spread rapidly in such cramped, unsanitary housing. People were always hungry. Heating fuel was scarce in the winters and few people had adequate clothing. Tens of thousands died from illness, starvation, or cold. Some people committed suicide to escape their hopeless lives. Every day children had to live on the streets. Many froze to death in the winter.

With both verbal and physical assault, and the legal and administrative restrictions placed on the Jews, by 1939, Jews were considered socially dead in German society. Jews lived in fear of terrorizing physical and verbal violence. Propaganda against the Jews was vehement and intense, ceaseless and repetitious. Physical abuse was encouraged and perpetrated against Jews, and the Germans were unrelenting. On September 1, 1941, the isolation of the Jews was symbolized by compelling Jews to wear a large yellow Star of David with the word *Jude* in black.

Such cruelty—which included mocking Jews, cutting beards off of Jewish men, burning people and synagogues—had no purpose other than to instill Jewish suffering. German people voluntarily and openly brutalized the Jews. Widespread enthusiasm allowed the genocide to proceed smoothly. People had a choice; they did not have to kill, but they chose to opt in. Peer pressure created perpetrators.

Another word for Holocaust is *Shoah*, the Hebrew word for catastrophe. The official persecution of Jews began in April 1933 when the Nazis initiated a boycott of Jewish businesses throughout Germany, and life for the Jews deteriorated. They were prevented from staying in motels, going to restaurants, theaters, and shops, or even sitting on park benches. Yet many Jews could not conceive of anything permanently altering their lives nor the enormity of Hitler's ultimate plan. It was this disbelief, even as persecution against them accelerated, that led many to remain home rather than leave Germany. Between September 1939 and August 1941, roughly 4000 people a month were killed under Germany's euthanasia program. On September 19, 1941, Germany invaded and captured the city of Kia in the Soviet Union. All the Jews of Kia were marched into a ravine, ordered to strip, then shot and killed. Thirty-three thousand Jews were massacred.

Concentration camp prisoners were usually killed by gas though other methods were used as well. Grizzly examples included shooting, hanging, starvation, being buried alive, being kicked in the genitals, inserting a hot poker down throats, locking people in a building then setting it on fire, and many more too horrible to mention. There were medical experiments as well, including breaking bones to see how they would heal, hitting heads with hammers, and exposing people to extreme heat and cold. People were infected with diseases then injected with a variety of drugs to see what worked. Transplantation experiments were conducted on limbs and muscles.

The extermination of the Jews had no political or economic justification, yet Hitler never made secret his intention to exterminate the Jews. The systematic way in which Jews were singled out for extermination made the Holocaust unique.

German women were brutalized, raped, murdered. The avatars

148

knew that there were terrible forms of suffering for German women, and these three young girls validated that. Up to half a million women in Berlin alone were raped or murdered. It was not just the Russian army that did the raping, though they certainly stood out as the most brutal. The French occupation soldiers were also notorious. American and British soldiers' behavior waivered between rape and consensual sex, blurred with the use of chocolate, lingerie, and cigarettes. The barter encouraged covert prostitution. Some girls suffered mass rapes and died from hemorrhage or internal injuries. Others were shot. The suicide rate of German women rose dramatically.

The avatars needed to return to their camps. They wiped their tears, hugged Karla, Maria, and Letta, and promised to return with more food and some clothing. Beth zipped back to Sandy as his Reconnaissance unit continued forward into Bavaria, but she decided she needed to get out of Germany for a while. She had to clear her head. The painful noise of battle, the disgust of people killing one another, the smell of death and gunfire, and the brutalization of women were overwhelming. Beth needed a break. Since she had been wondering about life back in the U.S. during the war, she decided this was a good time to visit her great-grandmother Lois in Ohio.

"Dude, I'm taking off for a while. I'll be back soon. Don't get shot or anything…"

"You said I would be okay."

"I said you'd live. I didn't say anything about not getting wounded."

In a blink, she was gone.

13.

THE STORY FROM HOME

Beth poofed onto the playground in Thompson Park in the center of East Liverpool, Ohio. The early April weather was cool, but it was a heck of a lot warmer than in Germany! As a simple breeze ruffled the new growth on the trees in the park, Beth thought about the people in small towns like this one who sacrificed many of their own necessities so that the men on the battlefront would have whatever they needed. Everybody pitched in for the war effort. Housewives gave their nylon stockings for the production of parachutes, and nearly everyone grew their own vegetables in victory gardens. Rubber, aluminum, and scrap metal were regularly collected. People waited in long lines with ration cards to purchase their allotment of food, clothing, and gasoline, and they stayed close to the radio at home to listen for news of the war. In spite of the rationing, Americans bought billions of dollars of war bonds to help finance military operations in both Europe and Japan.

Beth thought about the war and the horrors she had already seen. She knew that the United States media did a terrible job of covering the story of the atrocities towards the Jews in Europe, and no one knew about the horrors experienced by the women and children of Germany. People in and out of government were reluctant to accept that these events were actually occurring. Americans were divided on whether the U.S. should take part in the fight in Europe when it began in 1939. Most Americans wanted the Allies to win, of course, but they also wanted to keep the U.S. out of war. When Canada declared war on Germany, U.S. preparation began, building defense plants and giving the Allies everything except actual troops.

When Pearl Harbor in Hawaii was bombed by the Japanese in 1941, factories in the U.S. quickly converted to war production. For example, companies that made kitchen appliances now started to produce military weapons. Men joined military branches, or were drafted, and women staffed the war production plants. By 1943, Rosie the Riveter represented more than two million women who were working in shipyards and aircraft plants.

Rosie the Riveter

Beth knew that by now, in April 1945, life in the U.S. was consumed by war production, war news, war bonds, and war losses.

Lois was sitting on a bench in Thompson Park with her friend, Ann, during their lunch break from work. Beth landed in the playground about 50 yards from where Lois and Ann were chatting. They didn't see her less-than-graceful entrance, landing flat on her butt. The good news was that it looked like she had just fallen off the sliding board.

"Whoa! Ouch!" Beth was trying to get up, rubbing her very sore rear end. The women heard Beth holler, saw her on the ground, and ran over to help.

"Are you okay?" asked Lois as she took one arm and Ann took the other to boost Beth onto her feet. Lois noticed that the girl was dressed in a funny kind of military outfit, including pants, which Lois and Ann rarely saw on other girls. They were all about the same age, Beth only slightly younger.

"Yeah. Thanks. Wow! I landed hard!"

"Is there anything we can do for you? We have to get back to work but we can help you get somewhere."

"No... thanks, though. My name is Beth and, uh, I actually came here to talk with you, Lois."

"I need to get back to work," said Ann. "I'll leave you two for now." They all said goodbye.

"I have to get back to work, too, at the bank but you can walk with me," invited Lois. "What do you want to talk about? And how do you know my name?"

"Thanks... uh, okay, this is weird. I need to tell you some things that might freak you out a bit and it might take longer than a short walk. Can we meet back here at the park after work?"

"You have my curiosity and attention. Sure. I can meet you after work. I'll call my mother to tell her I'll be home late."

"You're married and you still call your mother?" Beth was surprised. In 2017, she hardly even spoke with her mother! And she was single!

"Of course! I live with my parents while my husband is away at war, and my mother isn't well. She worries about me."

"I get it. No problem. Let's meet back on the park bench later."

Beth and Lois met on the same bench a few hours later. The air was getting quite cold.

"Okay, I have three weird things to tell you, and I need for you to just listen before you say anything. Okay?"

"Okay." *Unusual*, thought Lois.

"Promise?" asked Beth.

"I promise."

"First, I'm a time traveler and I'm here from the year 2017." Beth paused.

Lois, looking somewhat amused, said, "Yes, that IS weird, but I believe anything is possible, so I'll go along with it." *Cool*, thought Beth. Then she took a deep breath.

"I'm, uh, I'm your, uh, great-granddaughter."

"My WHAT???" Lois felt her heart begin to race. "What???" she repeated. So much for amusement.

"Your great-granddaughter. My mom is your daughter's daughter." Lois looked stunned. Beth continued, "You said anything is possible! We call you Gran-Gran."

"Wait! I don't have children!" Lois was working up to a near panic.

"Well, not yet, but you will." Beth was trying to calm Lois. "That's all I'll tell you about the future other than you will have children and grandchildren and great-grandchildren, and you will live to be very old."

Lois thought for a moment then regained her composure. "My husband is in Europe fighting in the war. Does this means he survives? *Please* tell me he survives!" Lois stood up, almost hollering at Beth.

"Well, that's the third weird thing I need to tell you. I just spent the last two months with Sandy. The war is, like, total hell, but yes, he survives."

Lois didn't know whether to be happy or surprised or shocked, but for certain she was confused. Who *is* this strangely dressed young woman who seemed to be about her own age but says she's her GREAT-granddaughter? The only thing Lois decided she could do was ask questions and try to get some answers.

Lois asked Beth, "Why are you here? How did you get here again?" Beth hadn't yet explained the avatar thing, so she told Lois about computers and avatars and cosplay. Interestingly, Lois seemed to believe it was possible and was eager to hear more about the process. After Beth described the details of her ability to travel through time, Lois asked, "So why did you come here to East Liverpool? More importantly, why did you decide to go to Europe in the middle of the war? That seems awfully dangerous."

Beth answered. "My history teacher had my class do an assignment about whether or not the Holocaust—which is the killing of millions of people by the Nazis—really happened. I had heard Pop— your husband, that's what we call him, Pop—tell his army stories over the past few years. When he became an old man—you two live a really long time, by the way—he talked non-stop about his time in the army but he never really went into detail, especially about the bad parts. I wanted to see for myself, to know what really happened, and to understand why young men like Pop went to war, especially that war. So I did my avatar thing and joined up with him while he was on the ship going over to Europe. It was totally gross! He and everyone else were seasick like crazy. The boat became a giant barf-barge!"

"But didn't they notice you there? How did you just show up and not be a soldier?"

"When I time-travel, I can make myself any size I want. Here, I wanted to be my regular size so that we could chat comfortably. In Europe with Pop, I'm about the size of a cigarette and live in his jacket pocket. It's warm in there. You can't imagine how friggin'—oh, excuse me—incredibly cold it is over there. The funny thing is that Pop still thinks I'm a figment of his imagination to help him deal with his loneliness. Whatever works. No one else there knows about me. They just think he talks to himself... a lot!" Beth chuckled. So did Lois who was actually getting into the conversation and marveling at the thought that this very smart and courageous girl was her great-granddaughter! *I must have raised some amazing children*, she thought with a smile.

"So, Beth, why did you come here?"

"Well, Pop talks about you all the time. He misses you very much. And I got him to talk a bit about his family...."

Lois interrupted, "That's funny since he hardly ever talks about much of anything. He's so shy."

"He may be shy, but he thinks I'm not real so he talks about everything. Anyway, I wanted to know more about you and about what's happening in the United States during this wartime. I want to know what life is like for you, as my great-grandmother, and as a young new wife in Middle America. Are you okay with sharing that stuff with me?"

Lois thought about what she would, could, share and realized she actually needed to talk. She began:

"Okay. I hope this helps, or at least is interesting. 1943 was a very dramatic year in my young life of 17 years. Having just graduated from high school that June, I was enrolled at Ohio University because I was a budding journalist. I had worked on my high school newspaper and became the editor-in-chief in my senior year. I just loved to write about everything and anything. Unfortunately, my mother had become quite ill, diagnosis unknown at the time, so I had to remain at home to help care for her and do the cooking for my younger brother and my father. As a result, I enrolled at Steir Business College in town to further my business education that I had started in high school. I went in the evenings.

After several months, I graduated from there and I was placed in a new position at our local First National Bank as its first War Bond teller. What an impression Sandy's dad made on me and everyone in the bank when he came in carrying a grocery bag full of $2.00 bills that he had saved over the years and bought $40,000 of War Bonds. Wow!"

"Wow is right!" exclaimed Beth.

Lois continued.

"I often talked to myself on dates with Sandy because he was so shy. He sometimes brought presents for me, so my mother told me to be nice to him. I'd date him for six months or so then date others.

On September 8th, 1943, my mother was taken by ambulance to the Cleveland Clinic, 90 miles away, for further in-depth diagnosis. My father left for work and my younger brother went off to school and there I was, standing in the doorway of our home at 310 W. Fifth St., here in East Liverpool, all alone and feeling so forlorn and lonely. To compound matters further, that was also the day that Sandy left for Camp Gruber, Oklahoma, to start his tour of duty as a soldier in the army."

"THAT day really sucked!" exclaimed Beth. She asked, "How did your mom do at that clinic?"

"My mother came home after several weeks at the Clinic with the diagnosis that she suffered from ulcerated colitis, so she began receiving treatments from Milt Gottlieb, our family doctor. She did extremely well and was able to go back to work at the S&S Shoe Store that my father managed. When my mother was well, you would never know there was anything wrong with her at all, but when she had an attack, she was so sick she always had to be hospitalized." Lois stopped for a moment, took a breath, then continued.

"We're a very close-knit, loving family with not much money. I grew up during the Great Depression of 1929, and although we were eventually able to buy a home, there was not enough money to cover all the medical and hospital bills. So I went to work to pitch in financially."

Beth asked, " Were your parents born in East Liverpool?"

"No. My dad was transferred to East Liverpool from Youngstown, Ohio, where I was born, to manage the S&S Shoe store. I was eight when we moved. Both of my parents, Isadore and Frances Schon-field, were born in 1904 in the U.S., my mother in New York, my father in Pittsburg. My mother's parents, Isadore and Celia Tilkus Levy came to the U.S. around 1898, probably from Estonia. My father's parents, Aaron and Rebecca Krasnapolski came to the U.S. in the late 1890s from Poland."

Beth was confused. "I thought the last name was Schonfield."

"It is now," said Lois. "Their Yiddish name in Poland was Shanefeld. It got Americanized at Ellis Island to Schonfield."

Beth asked, "Got it. So when did you meet Sandy?"

"We had known each other since I was eight and he was nine. We met when my parents joined the B'Nai Jacob Synagogue on East 3rd Street. Sandy and I were in the same Sunday school class. My mother became the superintendent of the Sunday School while Sandy's dad was the Gabbai of the Shul. It was a match made in heaven and it worked!"

"What's a Gabbai?" asked Beth.

"It's a person who assists the Rabbi in running services in the synagogue," responded Lois. She continued. "We'd date then break up then get back together again because he always showed up on my birthday in April, bringing me a lovely gift, so I would be nice and start going out with him again. By the time we started school in the fall, we'd been dating for several months but I would again send him home for the same reason. He was just too shy and quiet!

During the months after Sandy went into the army, we kept in close touch and decided to get married on his next furlough. We wrote constantly, talked whenever we could get to a telephone. I continued to work at the bank. Thank goodness my mother was doing well. Sandy said he would come home on April 14th and we could be married then."

"Were you two going together when Sandy initially left for the army?" asked Beth.

"Not really. Sandy started writing to me soon after he left for the Army. This was the first time he had ever been away from home, except for a three-day Boy Scout camp he attended years before as a child. His letters were fun and we started a regular correspondence. All of the boys we knew eventually left for various parts of the military, so it was very lonely at home. There was no one to date, so I was going to the movies with my best friend Ann, or with Sandy's sister Fran, or with my family. But like everyone else, I stayed glued to the radio, at work and at home, for news of the war effort.

Sandy was at boot camp for only about a month when he was involved in a hand grenade explosion that put him in the hospital for the next few weeks. We continued writing regularly. In one letter I mentioned to him that I was baking cookies to send to several of our friends at different camps in the States. I didn't send him any cookies at that time because, being hospitalized and not knowing what was wrong with him, I didn't know if that would be appropriate. Well, I received a blistering letter from him saying, 'If that's the only thing you can write about, sending cookies to other guys, just don't bother to write to me any more.' I was shocked at his response! He's usually such an easy going fellow, and very quiet, to say the least, but I did not write to him after that and thought our friendship had been ruined. I was devastated, but felt I should honor his wishes." Lois sounded disappointed even still.

"Yeah. I've noticed that he's kind of the jealous type," said Beth.

"I'll say! One day in mid-November of that year, I had left work and met up with my Aunt Lil who was visiting from Youngstown. We did some grocery shopping and were carrying bags of food back to my dad's store, when at the very corner we had to cross to get on the same side of the street as the store, who should be standing there but Pvt. First Class Sandy Lebman all decked out in his Army uniform! I was so surprised to see him there! We stopped to say hello. I knew in my heart he was there because he knew that was the way I had to pass by. Being a gentlemen, he asked if he could carry our packages for us. He said he wanted to stop by to say hello to my folks at the shoe store. My mother loved him and I always knew I loved him, too, but Sandy and I were both so shy that we never expressed that verbally. Naturally my folks invited him to come home with us for dinner and a longer visit. That was the beginning of our future together, while he was home on that 30-day convalescent furlough.

We spent the next twenty-nine evenings together, seeing friends, going to movies, playing cards with my folks, and just enjoying each other's company. Sandy started asking me to elope with him while he was on that furlough. As much as I wanted to do that, being only seventeen years old and he only eighteen, I knew we couldn't do that without our parents' permission. Surely they would be against us not having a wedding. But it was wartime and so many young boys and girls were getting married because that was the only way they could cope with being apart during the war. I finally told Sandy that as much as I loved him, I would not elope, but I would be happy to accept an engagement ring so he would know I was 'his'!"

Beth remembered Sandy's story about the rings. Sandy had told his father he wanted to get engaged but didn't have any money for a ring. His dad sent him to his friend Jim Reese's jewelry store. East Liverpool was a typical small Mid-West town and everyone knew everyone else. Sandy went to see Mr. Reese. He didn't know what kind of ring to buy so Mr. Reese took twelve rings from the case and said, "Take these and let Lois pick out her favorite." Sandy went to the First National Bank where Lois worked and approached her teller station. He dropped the twelve rings on the counter in front of her and said, "Which one would you like?" So much for romance! Lois selected her ring then came out from behind the counter to give Sandy a sweet hug.

Lois said, "After the initial shock wore off, I chose this one." She showed Beth the ring. "It's not left my finger since that day, December 12, 1943, shortly before Sandy had to return to camp.

Both of our families were ecstatic that we had become engaged. We had a huge dinner at our house with Sandy's entire family there. He has a large family, three sisters and a younger brother as well as his parents."

Beth asked, "Are your parents friends with his parents?"

"Yes, all four of our parents are very close. When Sandy returned to camp after his furlough when we became engaged, I went to his folk's house every Friday after work. My folks would come there to pick me up. Sometimes all of us would have dinner together. During the following months, Sandy and I kept in close touch and decided to get married on his next furlough. We wrote constantly and talked whenever he could get to a telephone. He said he would be coming home on April 14th and we could be married then. I continued working at the bank. Thank goodness my mother was doing well. Life went on."

Beth asked, "What was your wedding like?"

"It was a ridiculous time. My mother and I drove to the train station in Pittsburgh to pick Sandy up and immediately came home for a wedding rehearsal at the synagogue. Even though money was terribly tight, my folks took care of the rehearsal dinner and Sandy's folks paid for all the flowers for the wedding, which was the usual thing to do. They also paid for the entire wedding luncheon that was held at the Travelers Hotel, the fanciest place in this little town."

A Jewish wedding takes place under a canopy, a *chupah*,

which is held up by poles in each corner by four invited people. "Of the four, one was my younger brother Jack, one was Sandy's younger brother Leon and the other two young boys were our friends, Josh Truxton and Eddie Firestone. They were all about the same size and close in age."

"Where did you go on your honeymoon? Did you even have a honeymoon?"

"We did. We went to Cleveland." Lois chuckled. "None of our parents would loan us a car so we had to take the Greyhound bus. Many of my mother's relatives came to our wedding by bus, so we waited until we thought they were gone before we went to the bus terminal. But when we got to the terminal they were all waiting to go on the same bus with us! But we made the trip to Cleveland for a short four-day honeymoon. We had the wedding suite in the Fenway Hall Hotel. Though it was the designated wedding suite at the Fenway, it consisted of twin murphy beds that folded up into the wall. What a surprise!"

Sandy and Lois were married on a warm spring day, April 16, 1944, just one week after Lois turned 18. Sandy's 19th birthday had been a month earlier. Beth knew their first anniversary was only a week away.

Lois visited Camp Gruber, Oklahoma, on several occasions during Sandy's training there. When Sandy was transferred to Ft. Riley, Kansas, Lois lived with him there for a short time until he received orders to ship out to go overseas. Lois went back home to East Liverpool. It was December, 1944. They'd been married for only eight months.

Beth asked, "Just wondering...why did you get married at such a young age?"

"Everyone gets married at our age but the war seemed to make it happen even faster. The men need someone to come home to. It's for their morale."

"What was it like for you to be at the army camps?"

"When I went to Camp Gruber a few weeks after we were married, it was the first time I had ever been on a train alone and it was a strange experience. I had never seen 'colored' drinking fountains and 'colored' toilets because we live north of the Mason-Dixon line, but south of that is very segregated. I felt like I was in a different world since I had never experienced that. Sandy met me at the train and took me back to camp. When we first entered the Day Room where the soldiers relaxed when they were off duty, they started whistling and hooting at me. I thought I would pass out! I was just mortified, but Sandy did everything he could to help me get acclimated to all the noise and excitement. He was able to sleep off base so we rented a little bedroom in a house in town where we stayed during my few days' visit. When I went back the next time, a few months later, the train ride was still a distressing experience, but at least I was able to cope with the soldiers' hoots and hollers. We stayed at the same house in town.

Sandy was sent to Ft. Riley, Kansas, that October. I got a leave of absence from work. The head of the bank was so accommodating that whenever I asked for time off, he always said, 'Go enjoy your soldier. Your job will be waiting for you.' I spent almost a month at Fort Riley with Sandy. We were supposed to be there for three months, but the war had escalated and he was called back to Camp Gruber to be shipped out oversees. We traveled together by train to St. Louis, but we had to change trains there. Sandy went on to Oklahoma and I came back home to Ohio."

"What's life like for you now?"

"Life is quiet. Everyone is on food stamps, and we have to ration gas, though we gladly take what we get in rations. I even have to stand in line to buy a pair of stockings for work. I wear dresses or skirts and blouses to work. Women just don't wear pants, except for the ones who work in the factories to build war equipment. I guess Rosie the Riveter is the one who started that pants trend. Oh my! And I have a victory garden. I grow my family's vegetables so we have plenty. I share with our neighbors as well.

The soldiers didn't leave Camp Gruber until mid-December. Sandy called me from Times Square in New York City on New Years' Eve before he shipped out the next day. I didn't hear from him for some time after that as he was on a troop ship going to the European Theater of Operation, as you know, but the first mail I did get was a little V-Mail letter. That thing was so hard to read but not impossible."

Beth knew that "V-Mail" was a single 4-1/4 by 5-inch sheet of paper. During World War II, cargo space on ships was saved for military equipment. Sacks of mail were massive and took up too much space. The U.S. Post Office devised a system to microfilm and then miniaturize letters—V-Mail. V-Mail saved precious ship space and still allowed troops to send and receive letters.

Lois continued. "That was the start of all the letters I've been accumulating since Sandy was sent overseas. I save every one of them in a Post Binder." *Good move,* Beth thought to herself. *Keep them all because my grandma needs them to write this story. Keep the pictures, maps, and other memorabilia, too.*

Beth asked, "Has Sandy sent you anything from the front?"

"Whenever he's able, he sends me dozens and dozens of flowers because there's nowhere else he can spend his money. It would be nice, though, if he would just send money home, but that isn't possible. I save every penny I make and buy war bonds with some of it so we will have funds to get our life started when he comes home."

Beth was curious. "How do you get information about the war?"

"We regularly listen to the radio for news of the war effort which sounds like it's finally taken a turn for the better, that we're finally on the offensive. Radio is our lifeline. I like to listen to Ernie Pyle and Edward R. Murrow, but I also like the shows of Kate Smith and Arthur Godfrey." Beth knew that the U.S. government relied heavily on radio programming for news and even propaganda. War correspondents such as Ernie Pyle and Edward R. Murrow brought stories home from the front, but newspapers were as censored as the soldiers' letters, so people rarely knew what was actually happening in Europe.

Beth asked again about rationing, fascinated with the concept. "Going back to rationing, what is rationed?" she asked.

Ration book 1944-45

"Everything," said Lois. "Sugar, gasoline, tires, nylons, even cuffs on shirt sleeves. Ration stamps are needed for these as well as for medicine. I have to stand in line for my family's ration book. We get one per family. The ration books are red, white, and blue. See?" Lois showed Beth the current ration book she carried. "Rationing is challenging because things run out before the month is up, especially sugar. At least we have our vegetables."

Beth thought about life for women in the U.S. during the war years of 1939 through 1945, when marriage rates rose and more unmarried women were having babies. Many women with no job training experience often served the war effort near military bases as prostitutes. Prostitutes actually enjoyed a fair amount of freedom in and around the military bases. At some bases, they were called "victory girls" because they engaged in sex with soldiers free of charge. In fact, penicillin was developed in 1941 to help soldiers survive venereal disease probably as much as for infected wounds from fighting.

Many women served in direct support of the war effort. While women were not included in combat positions, many served as nurses near combat zones. Nearly 100,000 women served in the Army and Navy, 23,000 in the Marines, and 13,000 in the Coast Guard. More than 1,000 women were Women Air Force Service Pilots but were considered civil service workers. (They were finally recognized for their Air Force service in the 1970s.) Both Great Britain and Russia also employed women pilots in their WWII air forces.

While Rosie the Riveter symbolized working women, soldiers preferred a different symbol, the pin-up girl, such as Betty Grable or Rita Hayworth, and the films of the 1940s were made for both morale and propaganda. *Casablanca, Mrs. Miniver, Lifeboat, Notorious, Best Years of our Lives, Wake Island, Battle of Midway, Guadalcanal Diary, Citizen Kane*, and *Destination Tokyo* were among the favorites. Walt Disney produced *Fantasia* (1940), *Dumbo* (1941), and *Bambi* (1942) as well as *Donald Gets Drafted* (1942), *Out of the Frying Pan into the Firing Line* (1942) and *Der Fuehrer's Face* (1943). Popular actors were Bette Davis, Gary Cooper, Humphrey Bogart, Katharine Hepburn, Joan Crawford, Cary Grant, Marlene Dietrich, Judy Garland, Ginger Rogers, Jimmy Stewart, Marlon Brando, Marilyn Monroe, Elizabeth Taylor, and Lana Turner.

Betty Grable's iconic pose for soldiers in WWII

In addition to the cultural education Beth was getting, she was fascinated by the cost of everything. For example, a new car cost $1,200; gas was 21 cents a gallon; a house could be purchased for $8,600; bread was nine cents a loaf, and milk was 62 cents a gallon. The average annual salary was $2,600, and minimum wage was 30 cents an hour.

It was time to go. Beth enjoyed her visit with her great-grandmother and looked forward to meeting her again in the future.

"Thank you for spending time with me and sharing information about your life. I need to get back to Sandy and the war."

"Thank you for visiting me, Beth. Please tell Sandy I love him and I'm waiting for him to come home."

"I will…"

Lois wrapped her arms around Beth and hugged her tight. "I know we really haven't met yet and so much will happen before we do in 60 years, but I already love you."

"I love you, too, Gran-Gran."

And then she was gone.

14.

APRIL 1945

Beth returned to Sandy after her visits with the girls in Mainz and with Lois in Ohio. It was early April and the 42nd Division was barreling through Bavaria. Target: Munich.

The Russian army was advancing to Berlin, liberating concentration camps along the way, though few people were found alive. The women and children who found alive were raped then killed. The Red Army brutalized as many women as they could find, especially in Berlin.

Sandy's unit wasn't in Berlin, though. They were in Wurzburg, launching assaults on what was left of the German army. After setting up close to the river, the men dug foxholes as German planes started dropping shells on the engineers who were building a bridge on which to cross the river. Two men were blown up. A shell landed near Sandy's foxhole.

"Dickie!!!" screamed Ketch. Dickie's leg was gone and blood was spurting out everywhere! Sandy could barely breath and Beth was screaming inside Sandy's pocket. "Dickie!"

"Dickie," yelled Sandy. "Hang on. The medics are close. Ketch and I are gonna get you there." Sandy and Ketch wrapped the stump that used to be Dickie's leg and carried him to the medic area. They never saw him again. Dickie bled to death. Sandy felt like he was hit in the stomach, the wind knocked out of him. Then he remembered Beth.

"Beth!" shouted Sandy. "You okay?"

"I'm okay. If you're okay, I'm okay." She was scared to death.

"I'm okay," responded Sandy. "It suddenly got scary out there! Damn!"

"Dude, breathe!"

"I'll try. It hurts…"

Both air and ground fighting was fierce. More than half of the houses and nearly all of the industrial plants in Wurzburg were destroyed. Several thousand civilians were killed or injured in that battle.

The city was already in ruins.

Sandy's unit received a direct hit. Dirt and body parts spewed into the air. Beth was sick. Soldiers' bodies flew up as if they were weightless. There were no survivors from the burned-out tanks. Men averted their eyes from the scorched human remains that were smeared across the twisted metal. One guy landed right in front of Sandy and Beth as they were showered with dirt from the explosions. The mangled bodies of Sandy's buddies laying in front of them looked like broken dolls. Sandy, Ketch, and Beth were paralyzed with horror. Nothing prepared them for this. They wanted to turn and run but there was no where to go. All they could do was cry.

Medics on the battlefront

The city of Wurzburg and the Homburg bridge that crossed the Main River were the Allied targets in April. The Main (pronounced Mine) is a tributary of the Rhine and the longest river in Germany. Wurzburg lay in a valley with high ground to the north. The men rowed boats into Wurzburg under heavy fire.

The huge Marienburg Castle was on the west side of the river. Nazis had painted the words 'Heil Hitler!' across the front of the castle. Sandy's unit replaced those words with signs that read '42nd Infantry Rainbow Division.' This was the first of thousands of Rainbow signs which marked every city, town or village the Rainbow captured or occupied.

The resistance was fanatical. Civilians, city police and firefighters joined with German soldiers in a desperate attempt to hold the city. A series of underground tunnels and destroyed stone buildings allowed the Germans the opportunity to establish a strong defense. As the U.S. infantry cleared the city block by block, the Germans went into the tunnels and popped up again behind the Infantry, but the Rainbow prevailed.

The soldiers found a giant stash of booze in a liquor warehouse, so much that they couldn't bring it all with them. They buried what they couldn't take with a plan to return later to the hidden caches. But they certainly took plenty of bottles with them.

By April 4th, Karlstadt and Muhlbach fell. On April 7th, the 42nd Infantry Division entered the ball-bearing center of Schweinfurt. Ball-bearings enable devices like planes, tanks, and cars to roll and are critical in warfare. The men of the Rainbow knew how important this town was to the German war effort. The approaches to Schweinfurt were heavily defended because the Germans had mustered every available weapon and soldier to defend the ball-bearing center, but the town was defended by youths not more than 17 years old.

By April 10th, all units reorganized for an attack on Schweinfurt, which was being bombed and blasted by artillery shelling. The Rainbow men fought day and night without stopping. The 5000 enemy soldiers in Schweinfurt fought to defend the town with their lives. Finally, on April 11th, the Rainbow captured Schweinfurt after hard bloody fighting. The attack continued against massive resistance, but the city belonged to the Rainbow.

U.S. soldiers learned of the death of President Franklin Delano Roosevelt on April 12th. There was barely a single serviceman who did not mourn the passing of their Commander-in-Chief.

Service to remember U.S. President Franklin D. Roosevelt

The next day, the Rainbow Division received orders to take the cities of Furth and Nuremberg. The men were tired from the fierce fighting day and night, but they kept pushing themselves to go farther, knowing that each day was bringing them closer to the end of the war.

On April 16th, Sandy and Lois's first wedding anniversary, Sandy was knee-deep in blood and guts on the battlefront.

During the early hours of April 16th, Sandy and the recons were sent out to determine the locations and strength of the German army for an attack on Neustadt. An ambush occurred, and the unit suffered many casualties. Sandy was hurt but kept pushing forward.

"You okay, Sandy?" asked Ketch.

"Pop, if you're hurt, you have to stop! The medics can fix you."

"Nah...just a scratch. I'm okay." Sandy was hit by flying shrapnel, but none of it went through his military-issued gear. It just knocked the breath out of him for a brief moment.

By April 19th, the Division had captured approximately 1,375 square miles of Nazi territory along with the city of Furth with a population of 100,000, all in just eight days of marching and fighting. In those eight days, the Rainbow seized over 7,000 prisoners and liberated more than 15,000 slave laborers. They advanced into the western edge of the historical Nazi shrine city of Nuremberg. The movement was so rapid that the planned defense by the Germans crumbled under the crushing power of the Rainbow.

Bombed out town in Germany

By April 23rd, as the attack continued, the heaviest fighting was in the vicinity of Dockingen where Sandy's unit battled its way through massive artillery, small arms, and flat-trajectory flak. Again, the casualty rate was high.

The mission for April 24th was to advance southerly towards Donauworth, clean up the resistance there, and establish a bridgehead for crossing the Danube. Though there was heavy fire, the advance was rapid despite poor roads, blown bridges, road blocks and challenging terrain. The attack progressed steadily throughout the day but by dark, all battalions reached their objectives. After the capture of Donauworth, Sandy's unit immediately initiated Reconnaissance for sites to cross the Danube. Under cover of darkness, assault boats and bridging materials were moved in. Beth knew she was witnessing a massive but instant construction event.

By April 25th, the Rainbow Division reached the Danube River and began crossing procedures. The ground was still frozen, making it nearly impossible to dig in. Dawn was breaking, revealing their exposed positions. Snow-covered fields stretched a thousand yards. "We don't have a chance out here," yelled Ketch to anyone nearby.

U.S. Recon soldiers building a bridge

On April 26, the infantry crossed the Danube River, heading for Munich. As soon as they reached the opposite shore, the men jumped out of the boats and ran as shells burst around them, diving in and out of ground craters until they were out of reach of the enemy fire.

The men desperately needed a rest. The month of April was non-stop fighting, and they were tired, dirty, and frightened. Many of their buddies had been killed or wounded. But resistance was minimal, and the men were able to reach the northwest bank of the Danube River.

From the woods, German fire grew in intensity, and German tanks moved forward in pairs. One pair would stop to shoot while the other pair moved past the first, alternating firing and movement. The Rainbow's easily discernible foxholes became targets for the oncoming Germans. Because of the frozen ground, the holes were shallow. In some places, German tanks simply rolled over and crushed some of the men.

U.S. Recon soldier with radio in foxhole

The German war machine was ground down by defeat and retreat. Tanks were short of fuel, artillery was short of shells, and many soldiers had gone unpaid for months. Morale was gone due to the nonstop defeats and destroyed hometowns. Yet they fought on with the courage of men with nothing left to lose.

The American soldiers carried on until they couldn't. One just sat down on a trail and cried, "I can't take no more of this shit!"

Ketch commented as they passed by, "If you get pounded enough, you're gonna break. I feel for that guy."

"Ya know, Germany is a beautiful country if you don't look at the destruction. Barbed wire everywhere, everything in ruins, totally and completely destroyed. Towns and cities, roads and bridges, everything is decimated. It's just a damned shame," Sandy added. "I feel for all of us. I hope we get out alive."

Unrelenting stress was profound. The men were beginning to go crazy. Nerves snapped sooner or later. Few believed they would survive to defeat Nazi Germany but they kept fighting. They had to cut themselves off from their emotions, stay detached, stay numb.

The advance to Munich continued. By April 28th, all units

closed in on their assigned areas. They seized Thierhaupten, Holzheim, and Neukirchen. Sandy was dispatched to make Reconnaissance of the bridges in the area while preparations were made for the advance into Munich.

Early in the morning on April 29th, about ten miles north of Munich, Sandy and the men in his car drove on dirt back roads as they paved the way for the Division to move into Munich. They began to smell something awful, something that reminded them of dead rotting meat. They found Dachau Concentration Camp.

15.

DACHAU

The internment of political prisoners in Germany gave rise to the need for concentration camps, the first of which was established on March 22, 1933, in the town of Dachau, about 12 miles northwest of Munich. The camp was located at the site of an abandoned WWI munitions factory, and the first prisoners were housed in the old factory buildings.

The renovation and operation of Dachau were used as the model for other concentration camps. New barracks had been built in 1937 by the prisoners themselves, allowing the camp to accommodate up to 500 people though over 30,000 were there at the time of the liberation. In the twelve years the camp was used by the Nazis, over 200,000 prisoners had been held there. There were over 31,000 registered deaths though many more had not been documented.

Dachau Concentration Camp was about the size of three city blocks, enclosed by heavy electrically charged barbed wire atop a massive stone wall. A moat inside the wall surrounded the entire camp, and seven watchtowers were placed at various points along the wall. Thirty-two wooden barracks and other buildings formed the perimeter of the area. Across the top of the main gate of Dachau was the phrase *Arbeit Macht Frei*, Work Sets You Free.

The prisoners at Dachau were from nearly every country in Europe. In addition to the many thousands of people killed in Dachau, there were 137 "Distinguished Prisoners" incarcerated there as well, including the former Austrian Chancellor Kurt von Schuschnigg, the former French Premier Leon Blum, the former Prime Minister of Hungary Von Kallay, and Protestant Pastor Rev. Martin Niemoeller.

Technically, Dachau wasn't an extermination camp like Auschwitz. It was a work camp of factories and repair shops that made a variety of products. But in the process, many prisoners were worked to death and thousands were shot, beaten, tortured, or starved to death, or they died of diseases or from medical experimentation. The crematorium was active twenty-four hours a day, burning human beings by the thousands. The exact numbers of the dead will never be known.

Human imagination could not prepare the Rainbow soldiers for what they were about to see.

Although it was at the end of April, the weather was very cold and there was a dusting of snow. Heading towards Munich, Recons Sandy, Ketch, Beth—who now considered herself a Recon—and the other men in the M8 found themselves driving slowly on a dirt road next to a thick tall stone wall topped with barbed wire. A guard tower high up on the stone wall was nearby but it seemed to be empty. No one had ever mentioned a camp in the area. The odor was sickening and the leaves on trees were covered with an ugly gray ash. The soldiers didn't know where they were, but they could feel that something was terribly wrong.

"This place stinks like the meat packing houses back home in Oregon," said Ketch as he pinched his nose.

"What *IS* this place, and what's that awful smell? Geez...." Sandy hollered to his men over the sound of the wheels of the armored car. Beth was becoming quite nauseated and buried herself deeper down into Sandy's pocket, covering her nose with her scarf.

"Dunno, Sandy. It might be a POW camp but we don't have that on our maps at all," yelled Ketch. "Let's follow the wall and see where it goes." The smell was sickening.

As they turned the corner at the end of the wall, they saw a train, or rather, about fifty rickety boxcars of a train sitting on a track, with bodies falling out of them. They couldn't comprehend what their eyes were seeing.

The train was parked on a railroad track close to the side gates of the camp. It was an assortment of odd boxcars, the floors covered with bodies. At least 100 bodies were jammed into each car. Thousands of men, women, and children were stacked up on top of one another in tangles of arms, legs, and blood. Most of the bodies were frozen. Some had been stepped on and crushed. A few managed to crawl out of the train only to die on the ground. Even fewer who had enough strength to try to escape had been shot. These people had been shipped without food or water or heat from other concentration camps to Dachau to be cremated.

One of the boxcars outside of Dachau Concentration Camp

Train outside of Dachau Concentration Camp

Both Sandy and Beth, faces covered with handkerchiefs to avoid the stench, were crying, feeling intense anger, wondering how people could possibly do this to other human beings. *What the hell was wrong with them???* Sandy radioed for the infantry to detour from Munich and get to this horrid place fast.

Beth asked, "Pop, if it's this bad on the outside of the wall, what in God's name is on the inside?" Sandy was thinking the same thing.

The camp was quiet. There were no sounds on the outside of the wall. Sandy climbed out of the armored car and walked over to the gate to see if he could observe anything or anyone inside. Guards suddenly appeared up in the nearby tower and began shooting. Sandy ran and jumped back up into the car.

"Rush the gate!" Sandy hollered. Sandy and Ketch, up in the turrets, opened fire and killed the guards. The gate gave way under the power of the car and the first U.S. soldiers—Sandy, Ketch, and the others in the armored car—entered the camp. To their utter horror, they saw fresh corpses, and wasted, diseased, starved prisoners who were dying before their eyes! In total disbelief, it was more than the men and Beth could comprehend. Everyone in the car was stunned. Nobody could talk. It was beyond imagination: They were at the crematorium.

Through his nausea and tears, Sandy asked himself, *Are any of these people my relatives?*

Dead people. So many dead people. The Rainbow was a fighting division and had seen death at close range every day for the last few months. This was different.

The prisoners who were still alive were happy to see the soldiers though their appearance was that of resigned hopelessness. Their gaits were slow, and many weighed only 70 to 80 pounds. Dysentery, typhus, and tuberculosis were rampant, adding to the putrid smell in the air. People were starved and nearly naked in the cold. With frail voices, many said they want to return home to families and friends, though neither homes nor families were there anymore. *So utterly unreal* thought Beth.

The smell of burning flesh clung to the soldiers' clothes. It got into their nostrils and throats so that their breathing was shallow through their mouths. Everywhere the soldiers looked were bodies, haphazardly stacked like fallen building blocks. Those still alive and strong enough to move about were hauling bodies away. That was their job, and the arrival of the soldiers didn't stop them. There was no food or water, and nearly all were wearing what looked like striped pajamas, torn and ragged.

Two of the striped pajama inmates were beating the crap out of another man, Beth saw, also in striped pajamas, thrashing him with a crutch. Sandy was about to stop the assault when someone explained that the "crippled" man was an SS Guard dressed in a prisoner's uniform to avoid being captured or killed. Sandy and the men left the aggressors to their own administration of justice. The barracks were built to accommodate about fifty prisoners each, though they were now filled with between 200 and 300 people who were stacked four or five to each bed. Many in the top bunks were too weak to move and were simply dying there, not even able to use the toilets which were two wood planks over holes in the ground over which one stood astride in full view without any privacy.

In the crematorium, bodies with paper tags tied to their big toes were stacked high to the ceiling like cordwood, twisted in heaps, awaiting the firing of the ovens. Before they were burned, the tags were pulled off. That was how a record of daily output was kept. The ovens, made by the Topf & Sohne company, were capable of burning more than 100 bodies a day. There was an overhead sign that read *wash your hands after work*.

As the soldiers walked around the area of the crematorium, they found a storage room with what appeared to be by-products of extermination: bags of human hair, teeth, eyeglasses, shoes, toys. There were also decayed, emaciated bodies, coldly and systematically tortured and killed. Piles of starved, twisted, racked bodies, some scarcely recognizable as human.

Help was urgently needed. Sandy called for medics and chaplains. They arrived, as did engineers to help purify the water and sanitation crews to deal with the filth. And food! Food was desperately needed. Many of the prisoners could not remember their last meal.

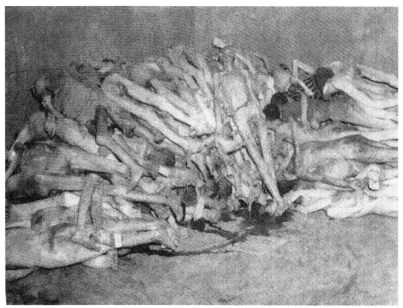

Bodies stacked by the crematorium

Furious by the sight of everything they saw, Sandy and his men tore down the Nazi flag from in front of the administration building and burned it. The American flag, the Stars and Stripes, was hoisted!

The American soldiers, now liberators, openly wept. Many vomited. All were dumbstruck. Some vented by firing into the guards who were still present. The stench of the place was overwhelming, and the sight of so many dead and emaciated human beings was beyond anything the men could have imagined. Sandy continued to wonder if any of the prisoners could have been his relatives. He remembered his father's tears from that day in 1940 when the letter that read *There's no one left* arrived. It haunted him.

It was all too much. The men were losing their minds. The army had trained them to fight, but it had not prepared them for this kind of psychological shock. Nothing could. It was a tragedy beyond comprehension. Bastards. Bastards. BASTARDS!!!

Beth knew that over the course of Sandy's life, Sandy would do his best to erase the abomination of Dachau from his memory, but the horror—and the traumatic shock—never left. The young men of the

42nd Rainbow Division, citizen soldiers turned liberators, now knew why they were fighting this war.

The town of Dachau, Germany, was a quiet little Bavarian country village about 12 miles outside of Munich, just up the road from the largest concentration camp in Germany. The citizens of Dachau saw and heard and smelled...and did nothing. They claimed they had no idea what was happening even when the smell of death was so prominent. They turned their heads away. They didn't want to get involved.

The residents of Dachau hung white bed sheets from their windows to signal their surrender. Soldiers gathered the people of Dachau and marched them through the camp. They made them look at what they refused to see for so many years. They made them dig graves and place bodies in them. Some were disgusted. Some became ill. Others acted like they were going to a park, laughing and giggling. One man was heard to say that the camp was "a great place. I like it for my mother-in-law." Sandy became so infuriated that he jumped the man.

"Sandy! No! He's not worth it!" hollered Ketch as he pulled Sandy off the man. Both Sandy and Ketch were crying.

Citizens of Dachau burying bodies

With the rest of the Rainbow Division arriving at Dachau, Sandy and the men in his M8 were ordered to continue on their Reconnaissance drive to Munich. As they left Dachau, no one spoke. No one could. They were each lost in their thoughts, stunned by what they had just witnessed, not understanding the events and sights and smells of this day. Over and over again the same cruel, brutal memories of carnage, torture, and disregard for human life would flash through their brains for the rest of their lives.

The American troops, and especially the Rainbow Division, had not intended to liberate a concentration camp, about which they had known nothing. They were there to conquer a country and defeat the enemy because that's what they were told to do. The Rainbow's encounter with Dachau was both accidental and decisive.

Sandy thought about the people he just saw, and especially the ones with the yellow Star of David on their ragged stripped pajamas. He wondered why they didn't resist, understanding, of course, that they actually did in their own way. The most passive heroism among the Jews in Dachau and in other camps was not to lift a hand against the Germans. That heroism was to resist feeling dehumanized, to practice the quiet everyday care for one's equally tormented peers, and to try to outlive the tormentors.

And now the American soldiers knew what they were fighting for, and certainly what they were fighting against. They were accustomed to violence and death on the battlefield, but nothing prepared them for this unspeakable place called Dachau. Sandy understood that the day at Dachau was more than a day of death and despair; it was also a day to celebrate, not with cheers, parades or fireworks but with thoughtful remembrance of when life prevailed over death. Dachau represented humankind at its absolute worst. The soldiers of the Rainbow paid the price of war with their innocence. Beth knew her Pop will never forget…

The next day, April 30th, the day after the liberation of Dachau and the fall of Munich, Adolph Hitler and his wife Eva Braun committed suicide in Berlin.

April 30, 1945
My Dearest Darling Wife:

I again have the chance of writing to you after just a couple of days this time which isn't half bad, is it? But in the couple of days, I believe you'll discover that we have made quite a bit of history.

I've really come a long way since I landed in Marseille, Darling. I went from Marseille to a little town called Serres, from there to Erkartawiller and it was from there we started our drive on March 15. We went to Wurzburg, from Wurzburg to Schweinfurt, from Schweinfurt to Nuremberg, and from there I guess you'll have to read in the papers where I am although you probably know by now. It's been a long hard drive but I hope it ends soon and I can take a long trip back to the States, although that's probably just a lot of wishful thinking.

We'll probably take a long trip but somewhere else, but I hope I'm wrong.

"Where do you think you're going to go, Pop?"
"I think they might send us to Japan."
"Nah, I don't think so." Beth knew that didn't happen.

Just think, the last day of April and I saw some snow flurries today. Just light snow but it was snow. But from where I am I can see snow all year round. When I think of you at home in summer clothes already it makes me feel good to know that you don't have to put up with this miserable weather.

Well, my Darling, they're about to serve chow and I can't miss that.

"I can't believe you still like this stuff."
"Look, it's what they give us and it's hot. And I do kind of like it."
"Aaaarrrggghhhh...."

I'll close for now loving you with all my heart.
Your loving hubby,
Sandy

16.

MUNICH

The Rainbow Division, with Sandy and the Recons in the lead, were ordered to leave Dachau and move into Munich, the cradle of Hitler's particular brand of insanity. While several divisions were on that mission, the Rainbow was to take the center of the city. The advance was quick. There was some enemy resistance, but the end was clearly in sight. Sandy and most of the 42nd Division met up in Munich; their stomachs still turned from what they saw at Dachau, and their hearts were hanging heavy. Without second thoughts, they seized houses from citizens for their own billets and slept in beds for the first time since the middle of March.

Tanks with U.S. soldiers rolled into Munich, meeting with nearly no resistance. There were thousands of both Allied prisoners of war and slave laborers cheering and welcoming the troops. German soldiers surrendered and were taken as prisoners.

Though now in rubble and debris, Munich had been a manufacturing center, and more than a fourth of the 800,000 population were slave laborers. As the first Rainbow men entered the city, the laborers went wild with excitement when they realized that the German army was not going to put up a fight. They broke into wine cellars and food storehouses for their celebration, sharing their take with the soldiers. White flags fluttered from windows throughout the city in surrender. Munich was a lawless town and the Division's job was now to restore order.

The capture of Munich freed prisoners of war of all nationalities who had been taken by the German army over the past five years. The Rainbow liberated 900 American prisoners of war and captured over 2,000 enemy prisoners. With this accomplished, the Rainbow continued the drive south to the border of Austria. Sandy and his men left Munich and headed toward Salzburg. They had traveled and fought for 260 miles during the month of April.

Freed prisoners in Munich

17.

THE END OF THE WAR

Sandy's unit headed toward Austria. The view of the Alps was stunning, but the clean air of the mountains could not take away the stench of death that lingered in the nostrils of the soldiers.

On the way, a large airport was discovered near the Austrian border. Nearly 1600 Germans, both male and female, were captured along with 100 aircraft and large quantities of military equipment. Eight hundred American soldiers, held as prisoners, were released. It was a good day's work.

On May 4th, the Rainbow Division reached Salzburg, Austria. The men were exhausted from the last six weeks of continuous fighting and marching. They looked forward to getting some sleep, eating decent food, and taking hot baths.

On May 7th, 1945, the German army formally surrendered. The war in Europe was over.

May 7, 1945
My Dearest Darling Wife:

Well, I guess it's all over except for the cheering. I'm sure glad as are millions of other people and I can assure you, it was none too soon to suit us. You'd be surprised how calm all the fellows are, Darling. You'd think that they would all be celebrating or something but everything is just as calm as if we were just on another break. The main reason for that is everyone is sweating out what's going to happen to us now. No one seems to know.

I guess I can tell you now of a few more places I've been. I've been in Munich as you have undoubtedly read in all the papers and heard on the radio, and in Dachau which is a very horrid place. I don't know if they printed the story of Dachau in the papers in the states or not, Darling, but if they did, they didn't describe that concentration camp there correctly because it is indescribable. There are hundreds of dead and dying lying all over the place which the S.S. had slaughtered, I guess I shouldn't go into that now, Darling because it's a very horrid thing.

They just brought some rum so maybe we're going to celebrate yet. There's a quart for two men, so I'd better finish this letter. I wish I could talk to you and I'd never run out of words. I'd just talk and talk. Anyhow, Darling, I think I'll close for now, so with loads of love and kisses, I remain only yours, Darling.

   Your loving hubby,
   Sandy

On May 8, 1945, 11 months after D-Day on the Normandy beaches in France, Germany surrendered, and the world celebrated the liberation of Europe from Nazi rule. The *New York Times* headlines read *The War in Europe is Ended! Surrender is Unconditional!*

May 8, 1945
Mein Lieb Frau:

   I'm sorry, Darling. I'm almost forgetting the American lingo because I've been speaking as much German lately as I do English. The above, as you probably know, means My Loving Wife.

   Today was a big day for the troops. They had the band here and quite an affair. They gave about ten or fifteen medals. I was awarded the Purple Heart. Yes, that's right, Darling. You didn't read it wrong. I never told you about it but when we were crossing the Main River, we were trying to get to a bridge to save it before the Germans blew it up and while we were going down the road, an SS man hit our M8 with a bazooka and I got a little scratch and for that I was awarded the Purple Heart. Our troop was also awarded the Bronze Star for its splendid work. So you see, we had quite a day.

   You ought to see the house we're staying in at present. It's really a nice little house. It's not far from the Austrian border and the Alps.

   I finally received some mail from you, Darling. I hadn't heard from you in three days and I knew it wasn't your fault. All of your letters are so sweet, all except where you stated that I hadn't done my share. Well, maybe I haven't but I've had plenty to do for a while. Don't get me wrong, Darling. I'm not getting sarcastic or anything like that, but when you see your buddies killed or wounded and gone through quite a lot of narrow escapes yourself, little things like that sort of irritate you. Do you get what I mean, Darling?

The fellows all want to know why I run around with my wallet in my hand, Darling. After I show them the pictures of you they clearly understand. I still don't know how I ever got so lucky. I really think you're beautiful, Darling, as if I don't tell you, and I don't see how it's humanly possible for me to stay away from you for so long. I'd give anything to be able to hold you tightly in my arms and press my lips firmly against yours, Darling, and with that thought in mind, I'll close, loving you with all my heart.

Your loving hubby,
Sandy

The War was over. It was time for Beth to return home. On the morning of May 9th, Sandy awoke early and looked for Beth. She was usually asleep in his pocket but Sandy could feel that she wasn't there. He checked his other pocket and his hat, then saw the note pinned to his pillow. He rubbed his eyes to read the small letters:

Dear Pop,
See you in 50 years.
I love you,
Beth America!

18.

The Return

In 2010, Sandy was invited to attend the 65th anniversary of the liberation of the Dachau Concentration Camp in Germany. He had not been back since Dachau was liberated in 1945, and Lois had never been to Europe at all. On April 29, 2010, they were there. At the main gate of Dachau, they saw a plaque honoring Sandy's Division. It read:

> *IN HONOR OF THE 42ND RAINBOW DIVISION*
> *AND OTHER U.S. 7TH ARMY LIBERATORS*
> *OF DACHAU CONCENTRATION CAMP*
> *APRIL 29, 1945*
> *AND IN EVERLASTING MEMORY OF THE*
> *VICTIMS OF NAZI BARBARISM,*
> *THIS TABLET IS DEDICATED*
> *MAY 3, 1992*

Sandy, like so many other WWII soldiers, did not speak about the horrors of the war, of the human destruction they found at Dachau, or of killing others. Sandy thought of himself not as a liberator but simply a soldier, doing his duty as he was told, who kept silent for over 60 years. But on April 29, 2010, Sandy was honored as a liberator.

The day of the ceremony at Dachau was gray and rainy but it didn't dampen the event. Sandy and Lois walked silently about the camp with the others until Sandy asked for some time alone. He went to the exterior wall, recalling the day, exactly 65 years earlier, when he and the men in his M8 armored car fired on the guards as they burst into the camp. And he remembered…

As Sandy choked back tears, not for the first time that day, he thought *this is the place.* He was at the side gate near the entrance to the crematorium. As he stood there, eyes closed, remembering what he had always tried to forget, he heard a small familiar voice. Beth America was on his shoulder, her arm wrapped around his head, with a red, white, and blue cape gently flying in the breeze like a U.S. flag.

"I was with you then, Pop. I'm with you now..."

And then she was gone...

THE END

EPILOGUE

Sandy left Europe on his birthday, March 13, 1946, and arrived back in the States on April 1st. It took several days until he was deactivated and able to go home on April 4th. He was 21 years old, weighed 127 pounds, served nearly three years in the 42nd Rainbow Division of the U.S. Army, and had not seen his wife since December of 1944.

There were no guidelines on how the returning soldiers might cope with the horrific things they had seen and done. Doomed to fight until they were killed, wounded, captured, or until they broke down mentally, they had few other choices but to lean on one another to endure and win the most destructive, bloodiest war in history.

How does one who faced his own mortality at such a young age communicate what that was like to someone who has never had to do that? They don't. They keep it locked away, suffering from undiagnosed and untreated post traumatic stress disorder, or PTSD, for the rest of their lives. The war never really ended for them. Over the decades, Rainbow soldiers did not talk about Dachau, not even with their spouses. The time they spent at Dachau was intensely personal and it destroyed their inner peace. They tried to forget, but Dachau could never be denied. It remained in the psyche of every soldier.

Sandy was diagnosed with PTSD in 2007, having lived with it for 62 years.

"Case the colors!"

With these words, in 1946, the flag of the 42nd Infantry Division, which had flown proudly during 114 days of combat in World War II and more than a year of occupation duty in Germany and Austria, came down. The 42nd Rainbow Division was officially deactivated. Today the Rainbow is the New York State National Guard whose members have valiantly served in the Middle East in recent years. They preformed well and received the prestigious Hanby Trophy, the first National Guard unit ever to do so.

Could it happen again, perhaps in the United States?

According to military psychiatrist Dr. Douglas Kelley, the Nazi criminals on trial at Nuremberg had several shared traits: enormous energy devoted to their work; a focus solely on the ends of their labors with little thought as to the means; and an intense desire for personal power and glory.

Could it happen again? The qualities that led the Nazis to commit such acts of horror exist in many people and they are not unique. In 1947, Dr. Kelley wrote that they are in every country in the world and have personality patterns that are not obscure. They are people who want to be in power. Dr. Kelley stated, "There are people even in America who would willingly climb over the corpses of half of the American public to gain control of the other half, utilizing the rights of democracy in anti-democratic fashion. Americans need to look closely at our own culture and politics if we are to avoid the extremism and brutality of the Nazis."

Most people's knowledge of World War II is shaped by the writings of Anne Frank's *Diary of a Young Girl* or books by Elie Wiesel or Viktor Frankel, and popular films about the war. Today, though, decades later, people view the Holocaust in the abstract, similar to the way slavery is now viewed: a series of horrors that had happened a long time ago in a world very different from our world today.

There are those who say that the Holocaust never happened. If that were true, then to where did six million Jews disappear during that war? Where did they go? That's why Beth wanted to go to Europe, to see the Holocaust for herself, then to make sure it's taught to, and understood by, people her age.... and by you.

We must remember the past and tell the story so that we may transform the future.

Author's Note: Beth

Beth was born in Dayton, Ohio, on May 16, 1995. Her great-grandparents, Sandy and Lois Lebman, traveled from Ventura, California to welcome the next generation of their growing family. I met them there from my home in Ann Arbor, MI.

After I held Beth and sufficiently kissed her entire face, I handed her to my mother Lois. I marveled that we had four generations of first-born women in the room that day. After checking all the appropriate appendages of her first great-grandchild, Lois handed Beth to Sandy who was seated in a large comfy chair nearby.

Sandy held Beth, kissed her, and rubbed her head. Then he looked into her eyes, mesmerized by the fact that this was his *great*-granddaughter. Suddenly, he had a flashback to 1945. He didn't know why. His eyes locked with Beth's, and suddenly there was a glint in the baby's eyes, a sparkle of knowing, of familiarity.

And then Beth fell asleep in her great-grandfather's arms.

Author's Note: Sandy and Lois Lebman

When the War ended in Europe in May, 1945, Sandy was in the Army of Occupation in Austria and Germany, hunting down runaway Nazis. He fell in love with a little town in Austria called Zell Am See, and often wrote to Lois that "someday" he would take her there. Being of working class, my parents never made it to Europe until that April of 2010 for the 65th memorial of the liberation of Dachau.

After the ceremonies, my parents went to Zell Am See, Austria, with my sister Barbra and brother-in-law Hal. My mother stood in front of the town sign, tears welling in her eyes.

She asked my father, "Sandy, do you know what today is?"

"Sure," he said. "May 2nd."

"No, " said Lois. "It's finally *someday*."

And then the 85 year-old Sandy and his wife of 66 years, 84 year-old Lois, kissed....

Sandy and Lois Lebman, 2010, Austria

TIMELINE AND VERY BRIEF HISTORY OF

WORLD WAR II

For complete information, access the accompanying
website for each item

1918

Nov. 11. World War I ends.
http://www.history.com/this-day-in-history/world-war-i-comes-to-an-end
Germany was defeated and blamed the Jews, among others, for the loss. The
defeat caused a depressed economy and violent struggles for control.

1919

June 28. Treaty of Versailles signed.
http://europeanhistory.about.com/od/treatyofversailles/p/overtofvers.htm
The Treaty prevents Germany from maintaining a military. In addition, Germany had to pay reparations to France and Britain.

1921

July 29. Hitler becomes leader of the Nazi party.
http://www.historyplace.com/worldwar2/riseofhitler/leader.htm

1923

Nov. 8-9. The Beer Hall Putsch. Hitler's attempt to overthrow the government
fails and he's sent to prison.
http://www.ushmm.org/wlc/en/article.php?ModuleId=10007884

1925

July 18. Hitler's book *Mein Kampf* (My Struggle), the Nazi manifesto, is pub-
lished. This book documents Hitler's ideas of anti-Semitism and German na-
tionalism.
http://www.history.com/this-day-in-history/mein-kampf-is-published

Hindenburg is elected president of Germany and stabilizes the government
and the economy.
http://www.britannica.com/EBchecked/topic/266224/Paul-von-Hindenburg

1929

Oct. 29. The Stock Market crashes and the Great Depression begins.
http://www.americaslibrary.gov/jb/wwii/jb_wwii_subj.html

Germany's unemployment doubles from three million to six million, and the government is falling apart. The SA Brownshirts terrorize citizens in the streets in many towns.
http://www.britannica.com/EBchecked/topic/514736/SA

1930

Sept. 14. Nazis become second largest political party in Germany.
http://www.britannica.com/EBchecked/topic/407190/Nazi-Party

1932

Nov. 8. Franklin Delano Roosevelt elected president of United States.
http://www.whitehouse.gov/about/presidents/franklindroosevelt

1933

Adolf Hitler becomes Chancellor of Germany
http://www.history.com/this-day-in-history/adolf-hitler-is-named-chancellor-of-germany

Feb. 27. Hitler convinces Hindenburg to issue a Decree for the Protection of People and State granting sweeping power to the Nazis, laying the foundation for a police state.
http://www.ushmm.org/wlc/en/article.php?ModuleId=10007888

March 20. First concentration camp, Dachau, established
http://history1900s.about.com/od/1930s/a/Dachau.htm

March 23. Enabling Act suspends civil liberties giving Hitler dictatorial power
http://www.historyplace.com/worldwar2/timeline/enabling.htm

April 1. Boycott of Jewish shops and businesses.
http://www.ushmm.org/wlc/en/article.php?ModuleId=10005678

April 7. First anti-Jewish decree, the "Law for the Reestablishment of the Civil Service"
http://www.jewishvirtuallibrary.org/jsource/Holocaust/ProfessionalCivilService.html

194

April 25. Laws enacted preventing Jewish students from enrolling in German schools
http://www.ushmm.org/wlc/en/article.php?ModuleId=10005681

April 26. *Gestapo* established
http://www.jewishvirtuallibrary.org/jsource/Holocaust/Gestapo.html

May 2. Trade unions dissolved
http://www.historylearningsite.co.uk/trade_unions_nazi_germany.htm

May 10. Public burnings of books authored by Jews or people of Jewish origin
http://www.ushmm.org/wlc/en/article.php?ModuleId=10005852

July. Laws enacted permitting sterilization of unfit parents, and euthanasia of people deemed defective
http://www.ushmm.org/wlc/en/article.php?ModuleId=10007057

July 14. Nazi party declared only party in Germany.
http://www.findingdulcinea.com/news/on-this-day/July-August-08/On-this-Day--Nazis-Ban-All-Other-Political-Parties.html

Nov 24. Nazis pass Law against Habitual and Dangerous Criminals which sends alcoholics and the unemployed to concentration camps
http://www.ushmm.org/wlc/en/article.php?ModuleId=10007499

1934

June 30. "Night of the Long Knives"
http://www.historylearningsite.co.uk/night_of_the_long_knives.htm

Aug. 2. Hitler becomes Furhrer. Armed forces must now swear allegiance to him. http://www.history.com/this-day-in-history/hitler-becomes-fuhrer

1935

May 25. Hitler violates the Treaty of Versailles and reinstates the military draft.
http://www.secondworldwar.co.uk/index.php/biography-of-adolf-hitler/64-hitler-biography-part-17

June. Compulsory abortions in certain instances begin
http://www.angelfire.com/mo/baha/nazis.html

Sept. 15. Nuremberg Laws enacted. Jews were defined as a separate race under "The Law for the Protection of German Blood and Honor."
http://www.jewishvirtuallibrary.org/jsource/Holocaust/nurlaws.html

Nov. 15. Germany defines who is a "Jew"
http://www.holocaust-history.org/questions/definition.shtml

Dec. 60% of Germany's youth belonged to the *Hitlerjugend,* the Hitler Youth.
https://www.jewishvirtuallibrary.org/jsource/Holocaust/hitleryouth.html

1936

March 7. Germans march into the Rhineland
http://www.historyplace.com/worldwar2/triumph/tr-rhine.htm

July 12. Sachsenhausen concentration camp opens
http://www.jewishgen.org/forgottencamps/camps/sachsenhauseneng.html

July 15. Buchenwald concentration camp opens
http://www.ushmm.org/information/exhibitions/online-features/special-focus/buchenwald-concentration-camp

Aug. Olympics in Berlin.
http://www.ushmm.org/wlc/en/article.php?ModuleId=10005680

Aug.. Nazis establish the Office for Combating Homosexuality and Abortions
http://www.ushmm.org/wlc/en/article.php?ModuleId=10005261

Oct. 25. Hitler and Mussolini form Rome-Berlin Axis
http://www.pacificwar.org.au/historicalbackground/HitlerfindsAlly.html

Nov. 25. Military pact signed between Germany and Japan
http://www.nizkor.org/hweb/imt/nca/nca-01/nca-01-09-aggression-13.html

1937

May. President Roosevelt signs the 1937 Neutrality Act,
http://www.pbs.org/wgbh/americanexperience/features/primary-resources/fdr-neutrality/

Oct. The SS transforms institutions for crippled children into euthanasia centers
http://www.ushmm.org/wlc/en/article.php?ModuleId=10005200

1938

April 23. Jews forced to eat grass on the Sabbath.
http://www.ukessays.com/essays/history/the-devastating-time-during-the-holocaust-history-essay.php

May. Flossenburg concentration camp opens.
http://www.jewishgen.org/forgottencamps/camps/flossenburgeng.html

Aug. 1. Adolf Eichmann establishes Office of Jewish Emigration in Vienna
https://www.jewishvirtuallibrary.org/jsource/Holocaust/imoffice.html

Aug. 3. Italy enacts sweeping anti-Semitic laws
http://motlc.wiesenthal.com/site/pp.asp?c=gvKVLcMVIuG&b=394669

Aug. 8. Mauthausen concentration camp opens in Austria
http://www.jewishgen.org/forgottencamps/camps/mauthauseneng.html

Aug. 17. Jews forced to change middle names to "Israel" for males and "Sarah" for females
http://forward.com/articles/182465/all-german-jews-forced-to-change-names-to-israel-a/

Oct. 5. Germans order Jews' passports marked with a large red "J."
http://www.ushmm.org/learn/timeline-of-events/1933-1938/reich-ministry-of-the-interior-invalidates-all-german-passports-held-by-jew

Nov. 9-10. Kristallnacht (Night of Broken Glass). 1400 synagogues are attacked, burnt, and/or desecrated and tens of thousands are sent to concentration camps.
http://www.ushmm.org/outreach/en/article.php?ModuleId=10007697

Nov. 12. 26,000 Jews arrested and sent to concentration camps
http://www.p12.nysed.gov/ciai/socst/ghgonline/units/6/documents/Unit6DNewspaper.pdf

Nov. 15. all Jewish pupils expelled from German schools
http://histclo.com/schun/country/ger/era/tr/jew/ned-jew.html

1939

Time magazine prints its 1938 Man of the Year edition choosing Adolf Hitler
http://content.time.com/time/magazine/article/0,9171,760539,00.html

May. The S.S. St. Louis, a ship with 930 Jewish refugees, is turned away by the United States, Cuba, and other countries. Forced to return to Europe.
http://www.jewishvirtuallibrary.org/jsource/Holocaust/stlouis.html

May 10. Germany invades Holland, Belgium and France
http://www.history.com/this-day-in-history/as-germany-invades-holland-and-belgium-winston-churchill-becomes-prime-minister-of-great-britain

May 18. Woman's concentration camp established at Ravensbrueck.
http://www.ushmm.org/wlc/en/article.php?ModuleId=10005199

Aug. 8. Battle of Britain begins
http://www.history.com/topics/world-war-ii/battle-of-britain

Sept. 1. World War II begins when Germany invades Poland.
http://history1900s.about.com/od/worldwarii/a/wwiistarts.htm

Sept 3 1939. Great Britain and France declare war on Germany
http://www.history.com/this-day-in-history/britain-and-france-declare-war-on-germany

Sept. 5 United States proclaims neutrality.
http://www.worldwar2history.info/in/USA.html

Sept 21. Ghettos established in German-occupied Poland.
http://www.ushmm.org/outreach/en/article.php?ModuleId=10007706

Sept 27. German troops capture Warsaw
http://en.wikipedia.org/wiki/Siege_of_Warsaw_(1939)

Nov. 23. Jews in German-occupied Poland forced to wear yellow Star armband
http://www.geschichteinchronologie.ch/judentum-aktenlage/hol/EncJud_Jewish-badge-and-armbands-1939-1945-ENGL.html

Nov. 28. First ghetto in Poland established in Piotrków
http://www.holocaustresearchproject.org/nazioccupation/piotrkow.html

1940

May 7. Lodz Ghetto: 165,000 people in 1.6 square miles.
http://www.jewishvirtuallibrary.org/jsource/Holocaust/lodz.html

May 10. Nazis invade France, Belgium, Luxembourg and the Netherlands.
http://www.ushmm.org/wlc/en/article.php?ModuleId=10005181

May 20. Auschwitz concentration camp established
http://www.ushmm.org/wlc/en/article.php?ModuleId=10005189

June 22. France surrenders.
http://www.eyewitnesstohistory.com/francesurrenders.htm

Sept. 7 German blitz against England begins
http://www.history.com/this-day-in-history/the-blitz-begins

Nov. 5. Roosevelt is re-elected as US president.
http://www.history.com/this-day-in-history/fdr-re-elected-president

Nov. 16. Warsaw Ghetto sealed with 500,000 people enclosed.
http://www.ushmm.org/learn/timeline-of-events/1939-1941/warsaw-ghetto-sealed

1941

Jan. 21-26. Anti-Jewish riots in Romania, hundreds of Jews butchered.
http://www.jewishvirtuallibrary.org/jsource/vjw/romania.html

March. Adolf Eichmann appointed head of Jewish affairs of the Reich Security Main Office
http://www.ushmm.org/wlc/en/article.php?ModuleId=10007412

June 22. Germany invades the Soviet Union.
http://www.ushmm.org/wlc/en/article.php?ModuleId=10005164

July 31. Heydrich appointed by Göring to implement the "Final Solution".
http://www.ushmm.org/wlc/en/article.php?ModuleId=10007328

July/Aug. Thousands of Russians and Jews are murdered by the Einsatzgruppen (extermination squads), including:

     5,200 Jews murdered in Byalistok
     2,000 Jews murdered in Minsk
     5,000 Jews murdered in Vilna
     5,000 Jews murdered in Brest-Litovsk
     5,000 Jews murdered in Tarnopol
     3,500 Jews murdered in Zloczow
     11,000 Jews murdered in Pinsk
     14,000 Jews murdered in Kamenets Podolsk
     12,287 Jews murdered in Kishinev

http://www.ushmm.org/wlc/en/article.php?ModuleId=10005130

Aug 20. Approximately 4300 Jews deported from Paris to concentration camp.
http://www.yadvashem.org/yv/en/holocaust/france/deportations.asp

Sept. 1. Jews in Third Reich must wear yellow Star of David
http://motlc.wiesenthal.com/site/pp.asp?c=gvKVLcMVIuG&b=394917

Sept. 3. First gassing at Auschwitz
http://www.deathcamps.org/occupation/auschwitz.html

Sept 28-29. 34,000 Jews massacred at Babi Yar
http://www.history.com/this-day-in-history/babi-yar-massacre-begins

Oct. Establishment of Birkenau concentration/extermination camp
http://remember.org/camps/birkenau/bir-introduction.html

Dec 7. Japanese attack Pearl Harbor.
http://www.history.navy.mil/faqs/faq66-1.htm

Dec 8. Chelmno (Kulmhof) extermination camp begins operations: 340,000 Jews, 20,000 Poles and Czechs murdered by April 1943.
http://www.jewishgen.org/forgottencamps/camps/chelmnoeng.html

Dec. 8. United States and Britain declare war on Japan.
http://www.history.com/this-day-in-history/the-united-states-declares-war-on-japan

Dec 11. U.S. declares war on Germany
http://en.wikipedia.org/wiki/United_States_declaration_of_war_upon_Germany_(1941)

Dec. 27. U.S. rationing begins.
http://www.ameshistory.org/exhibits/events/rationing.htm

1942

Jan 20. Wannsee Conference in Berlin where Heydrich outlines plan to murder Europe's Jews.
http://en.wikipedia.org/wiki/Wannsee_Conference

March 17. Extermination begins in Belzec. By end of 1942, 600,000 Jews murdered.
http://www.deathcamps.org/belzec/belzec.html

April 1 Japanese-Americans in U.S. center relocation camps.
http://en.wikipedia.org/wiki/Internment_of_Japanese_Americans

May. Extermination by gas begins in Sobibor killing center. By Oct. 1943, 250,000 Jews murdered.
http://www.ushmm.org/wlc/en/article.php?ModuleId=10005192

June. Jewish partisan units established in the forests of Byelorussia and the Baltic States.
http://www.ushmm.org/outreach/en/article.php?ModuleId=10007743

July 22. Germans establish Treblinka concentration camp
http://www.ushmm.org/wlc/en/article.php?ModuleId=10005193

July. 26. first American forces arrive in Great Britain.
http://www.historyplace.com/worldwar2/timeline/ww2time.htm

Sept. 13. Battle of Stalingrad begins.
http://en.wikipedia.org/wiki/Battle_of_Stalingrad

1943

Jan. 27. First U.S. bombing raid on Germany targets Wilhelmshaven.
http://en.wikipedia.org/wiki/Bombing_of_Wilhelmshaven_in_World_War_II

Feb. About 80 to 85 percent of the Jews who would die in the Holocaust have already been murdered.

Feb. 2. German Army surrenders at Stalingrad
http://www.history.com/this-day-in-history/germans-surrender-at-stalingrad

March. Liquidation of Krakow ghetto
http://www.ushmm.org/wlc/en/article.php?ModuleId=10005169

April 19. Warsaw Ghetto revolt begins
http://www.ushmm.org/wlc/en/article.php?ModuleId=10005188

Oct.-Nov. Rescue of the Danish Jewry
http://www.ushmm.org/outreach/en/article.php?ModuleId=10007740

1944

June 6. D-Day: Allied invasion at Normandy.
http://www.army.mil/d-day/

July 20. German officers attempt to assassinate Hitler.
http://www.ushmm.org/learn/timeline-of-events/1942-1945/attempt-to-assassinate-hitler

Aug. 25. German forces surrender in Paris
http://www.historylearningsite.co.uk/liberation_of_paris.htm

Sept. 3. Anne Frank deported the Auschwitz.
http://www.ushmm.org/wlc/en/article.php?ModuleId=10005210

Oct. 23. Paris liberated.
http://www.history.com/this-day-in-history/liberation-of-paris

Dec. Battle of the Bulge
http://www.army.mil/botb/

1945

Jan. 17. Evacuation of Auschwitz
http://www.rense.com/general69/evac.htm

Jan. 25. Death marches for inmates of concentration camps
http://www.ushmm.org/wlc/en/article.php?ModuleId=10005162

Feb. 23. flag raised by U.S. Marines on Mount Suribachi in Iwo Jima.
http://en.wikipedia.org/wiki/Iwo_Jima

April 12. Pres. Roosevelt dies. Truman becomes president.
http://learningenglish.voanews.com/content/american-history-roosevelts-death-makes-truman-president-126294003/116164.html

April 21. Soviets reach Berlin.
http://www.eyewitnesstohistory.com/berlin.htm

April 29. Liberation of Dachau.
http://www.nizkor.org/hweb/camps/dachau/dachau-01.html

April 30. Hitler commits suicide
http://www.history.com/this-day-in-history/adolf-hitler-commits-suicide-in-his-underground-bunker

May 7. Unconditional surrender of Germany
http://www.history.com/this-day-in-history/germany-surrenders-unconditionally-to-the-allies-at-reims

May 8. victory in Europe, V-E Day.
http://www.history.com/this-day-in-history/v-e-day-is-celebrated-in-american-and-britain

Aug. 6. Bombing of Hiroshima
http://www.history.com/topics/world-war-ii/bombing-of-hiroshima-and-nagasaki

Aug. 9. Bombing of Nagasaki
http://www.history.com/topics/world-war-ii/bombing-of-hiroshima-and-nagasaki

Aug. 15. V-J Day: Victory over Japan proclaimed
http://www.history.com/topics/world-war-ii/v-j-day

Sept. 2. Japan surrenders; end of World War II
http://en.wikipedia.org/wiki/End_of_World_War_II_in_Asia

Oct. 24. United Nations is created
http://www.history.com/this-day-in-history/the-united-nations-is-born

Oct. 20. Nuremberg war crimes trials begin.
http://www.historyplace.com/worldwar2/timeline/nurem.htm

1947

The United Nations establishes a Jewish homeland in British-controlled Palestine, which becomes the State of Israel in 1948.
http://www.history.com/this-day-in-history/state-of-israel-proclaimed

RESOURCES AND REFERENCES

Abzub, R. H. (1985). Inside the Vicious Heart: Americans and the Liberation of Nazi Concentration Camps. Oxford University Press

Afterman in Europe: War on the Beaches. *Time* Magazine. (V. XLV, No. 24, June 11, 1945).

Bohjalian, C. (2008). Skeletons at the Feast. NY: Crown.

Daley, H. C. (1946). 42nd Rainbow Infantry Division: Combat History of World War II. Baton Rouge, LA: Army & Navy Publishing Company

El-Hai, J. (2013). The Nazi in the Psychiatrist: Herman Goering, Dr. Douglas M. Kelley, and a Fatal Meeting of Minds at the End of World War II. NY: Public Affairs.

Fink-Whitman, R. (2013). *The Mandate Video.*
http://www.teacheroz.com/WWIIHomefront.htm

Follet, K. (2012). Winter of the World. Book 2: Century Trilogy. NY: Penguin

Foss, C. F. (Ed.) (2002). The Encyclopedia of Tanks and Armored Fighting Vehicles - The Comprehensive Guide to Over 900 Armored Fighting Vehicles From 1915 to the Present Day. MI: Thunder Bay Press

Glasser, R. J. (2011), Broken Bodies, Shattered Minds. NY: History Publishing

Goldhagen, D. J. (1996). Hitler's Willing Executioners: Ordinary Germans and the Holocaust. New York: Alfred A. Knopf.

Gun, N. E. (1966). The Day of the Americans. New York: Fleet Press Corp

Helen, W. & Gregory, D. (2008). Jungvolk: The story of a Boy Defending Hitler's Third Reich. Drexel Hill, PA: Casemate Publishing.

Heller, R. (2015). The Unlikely Governor: An Immigrant's Journey from Wartime Germany to the Federal Reserve Board. Maybridge Press

Hold at All Cost: 42nd Rainbow Division Prisoners of War. (2004). MN: Rainbow Division Veterans Memorial Foundation.

Kater, M. H. (2004) Hitler Youth. Cambridge, MA: Harvard University Press.

Kershaw, A. (2012). The Liberator. NY: Crown

Kershaw, A. (2015). Avenue of Spies. New York: Crown Publishers.

Kinsey, S. F. (2012). Yours 'til the End. Destin, Florida: Bush Publishing & Associates.

Kramer, C. (2009). Clara's War: One Girl's Story of Survival. New York: HarperCollins.

Levinson, L. (2011). Gated Grief: The Daughter of a GI Concentration Camp Liberator Discovers a Legacy of Trauma. WI: Cable Publishing.

Lowe, W. (2013). Hitler's Furies. German Women in the Nazi Killing Fields. NY: Houghton Mifflin.

Medoff, R. (Dec. 20, 2015) The American Papers that Praised Hitler. *The Daily Beast.* http://www.thedailybeast.com/articles/2015/12/20/when-america-s-media-cozied-up-to-hitler.html?via=mobile&source=email

MessyNessy. (2015). The Anti-Nazi Teen Gang that Beat Up Hitler Youth and Danced to Jazz http://www.messynessychic.com/2015/10/29/the-anti-nazi-teen-gang-that-beat-up-hitler-youth-and-danced-to-jazz/

Monthly Reports of Operations, Headquarters, 242d Infantry Regiment, 8 December 1944 through 10 May 1945, United States National Archives and Records Administration (NARA), College Park, MD.

Picoult, J. (2013). The Storyteller. New York: Simon & Schuster

Power, S. (2013). A Problem from Hell: America and the Age of Genocide. NY: Basic Books.

Rainbow Reveille (May 11, 1945). From Strasburg to Salzburg: 42d adds to past glories in dash across Germany. 42nd Rainbow Division Foundation.

Rominger, L. M. & James, M. (2003) Tour of Duty: 50 Inspiring Stories from our Men and Women in the Armed Forces. B.C., Canada: Fairwinds Press

Rush, R. S. (2003). The U.S. Infantry Man in World War II. Oxford, United Kingdom: Osprey Publishing.

Schaeffer, C. (2014). Assignment Asking Students Whether the Holocaust was Real Results in Disturbing Answers and Grades. http://www.ijreview.com/2014/07/156918-assignment-asking-students-whether-holocaust-real-results-disturbing-answers-grades/

Setterington, K. (2013). Branded by the Pink Triangle. Toronto, Ontario, Canada: Second-Story Press.

Shirer, W. L. (1960). The Rise and Fall of the Third Reich. The History of Nazi Germany. New York: Simon & Schuster.

Singer, A. (2014). *Night will Fall*. HBO: http://www.hbo.com/documentaries/night-will-fall/synopsis.html

Sites, K. (2013). The Things They Cannot Say. New York: HarperCollins.

Smith, M. J. (1995). Dachau: The Harrowing of Hell. State University of New York Press.

Sorge, M. K. (1986). The Other Price of Hitler's War: German Military and Civilian Losses Resulting from World War II. CT: Greenwood press.

Stanton, S. L., (1995). U.S. Army Uniforms of World War II. Stackpole Books

Strom, K. A. (Nov. 13, 2012). A Memorial for the Millions of German Women and Girls Who Were Raped and Pillaged by the WWII Allied "Liberators". http://justice4germans.com/2012/11/13/a-memorial-for-the-millions-of-german-women-and-girls-who-were-raped-and-pillaged-by-the-wwii-allied-liberators/

Survivors Speak Out. (1989). Jerusalem, Israel: Geffen Publishing House.

Tatelbaum, I. B. (2004). To Our Eyes: Children Witnessed the Holocaust. Jerusalem, Israel: Yad Vashem

U.S. Army Center of Military History. http://www.history.army.mil

Vannoy, A. (Feb, 2001). Operation Nordwind: U.S. Army's 42nd Infantry Division Stood Its Ground During World War II. *World War II Magazine*

Wolf, C. (2013). Soldiers' Letters Home. World War II Letters from 1942 to 1945. Self-published.

Websites:

http://www.jewishgen.org/forgottencamps/general/timeeng.html

http://wiki.answers.com/Q/What_role_did_German_children_play_in_World_War_2#page1

http://www.dailymail.co.uk/news/article-509510/What-German-children-played-World-War-Two--Nazi-party-sticker-books.html

http://m.spiegel.de/international/spiegel/a456835.html#spRedirectedFrom=w
ww&referrrer=http://search.yahoo.com/mobile/s?ei=UTF-
8&_tsrc=apple&r=web_filter&r=web_filter&fr2=p&p=german+children+of+
wwii+

http://ezinearticles.com/?Life-as-a-Child-in-Germany-During-World-War-
II&id=562296

http://www.historylearningsite.co.uk/children_and_world_war_two.htm

http://www.dailymail.co.uk/news/article-476361/German-children-played-
Bombers-England-boardgames-WWII.html

http://m.spiegel.de/international/germany/a680354.html#spRedirectedFrom=w
ww&referrrer=http://search.yahoo.com/mobile/s?rewrite=72&.tsrc=apple&fir
st=1&p=german+women+of+wwii+books&pintl=en&pcarrier=Verizon&pmc
c=310&pmnc=000

http://www.teacheroz.com/WWIIHomefront.htm

http://www.mainpost.de/regional/wuerzburg/3-April-1945-Tod-am-
Main;art735,6995227

http://www.youtube.com/watch?v=4V4bmm6yJMw

Other sources

National Military Archives
http://www.archives.gov/st-louis/

New York Public Library
http://www.nypl.org

About the Author

Ronni Sanlo
2016

Dr. Ronni Sanlo is the author of *The Soldier, the Avatar, and the Holocaust* and *The Purple Golf Cart: The Misadventures of a Lesbian Grandma* as well as many academic publications. She is the Director Emeritus of the UCLA Lesbian Gay Bisexual Transgender Center (LGBT) Center and a frequent keynote speaker and consultant. Now retired, Dr. Sanlo was the Senior Associate Dean of Students and professor/director of the UCLA Masters of Education in Student Affairs and served on the Higher Education faculty at California State University Fullerton. Prior to her tenure at UCLA, Ronni directed the University of Michigan LGBT Center, and, formerly, was an HIV/AIDS epidemiologist in Florida.

Ronni earned a bachelor's degree from the University of Florida, and a masters and doctorate in education from the University of North Florida in Jacksonville. She is the founding chair of the Consortium of Higher Education Lesbian Gay Bisexual Transgender Resource Professionals, and is the originator of the award-winning Lavender Graduation, a commencement event that celebrates the lives and achievements of graduating LGBT college students.

Ronni was born in East Liverpool, Ohio, and grew up in North Miami Beach, Florida, where she attended Temple Beth Torah. She continues to research and write, focusing primarily on LGBT history which is the foundation for the award-winning 2014 documentary *Letter to Anita*.

When Ronni isn't playing passionate but rotten golf, she is writing, kayaking, traveling, or just enjoy life. She lives with her wife, Dr. Kelly Watson, in Palm Springs, CA, and Sequim, WA.

Contact Ronni for book signings, speaking engagements, discussions, or just to say hello at ronni@ronnisanlo.com.

Autographed copies of this book may be purchased at
www.ronnisanlo.com